I0141531

Bobbi Mercer

RETURN TO PURE WORSHIP

Christianity and the Traditions of Men

RETURN TO PURE WORSHIP

Christianity and the Traditions of Men

Bobbi Mercer

Mercy Publishing
Bigfork, Montana

Copyright © 2015 Mercy Publishing

All rights reserved. Except for brief quotations in articles, other publications, book reviews, and blogs, no part of this book may be reproduced in any manner without prior written permission from the publishers. For information, write,

bobbimercer99@yahoo.com

Unless otherwise stated, scripture quotations are from *The King James Version*, copyright © 1942.

RETURN TO PURE WORSHIP Christianity and the Traditions of Men

ISBN-13: 978-0692422243

ISBN-10: 0692422242

Table of Contents

HEALING THE HURT OF THE DAUGHTER OF MY PEOPLE

Dead Flies in the Ointment Cause the Anointing to Stink

INTRODUCTION Not Without Cost!

There is a principle in the Spirit realm regarding cost. If something doesn't cost you much, it is not valued as much or valued at all, verses something that costs you a great deal. You treasure something when it has a "high price" on it.

On November 1, 1996 He commanded: Matthew 19:21: "IF thou wilt be perfect, go and sell that thou hast, and give to the poor, and thou shalt have treasure in heaven; and come and follow ME."

It took my two sons and me a week to get rid of everything. Every day when He would wake me up at 3:22 a.m., He would instruct me of what we needed to get rid of and how to do it.

We had to believe for EVERYTHING: food, money for the utilities, gasoline, our health, our daily existence!

I had a son who was 11, and a son who was two., three cats and two goldfish! Living in an apartment with no furniture or extra comfort stuff (including clothing-bear minimum) and sometimes no food (remember the children of

Israel, after physically leaving Egypt, they too, had testings of no food and sometimes no water for a short while. NOTE: The Lord of Hosts Knows how long a test can last); is quite humbling and a true experience of FIRE!

We lived that way for a great, great while. September 2001 was the beginning of a restoration of "stuff".

One afternoon, in 1997, I was laying on the floor, BEGGING the Lord to be made free and to deliver me and my sons. His Word came very swiftly and strong: "NOT WITHOUT COST!" Immediately after that strong rebuke, I turned to the window, and there was a shadow of a cross on the wall. I began to weep as I knew what the Holy Spirit was saying by showing me that cross.

This small book cost Heaven everything. Jesus laid down His Glory and took on humanity and then "became sin" for my salvation. These precious truths that have been revealed to me, AND embraced, by His Grace and Mercy, have cost me everything too. But like Paul wrote in Philippians 3:8, 10 -"Yea doubtless, I count all things but loss for the excellency of the knowledge of Christ Jesus my Lord: for whom I have suffered the loss of all things, and do count them but dung, that I may win Christ............

That I may know Him and the power of His resurrection, and the fellowship of His sufferings, being made conformable unto His Death."

Romans 8:18....."For I reckon that the sufferings of this present time are not worthy to be compared with the GLORY which shall be revealed in us......Amen and Amen.

So as you read this book, "Remember", the Lord warned: Count the Cost before you start.....

Luke 9:62- "And Jesus said unto him, No man, having put his hand to the plough, and looking back, is fit for the Kingdom of God.:" Luke 14:28, 33, 34, 35..."For which of you, intending to build a tower, sits not down first, and counteth the cost, whether he has sufficient to finish it?...So likewise, whosoever he be of you that forsake not all that he hath, he cannot be my disciple. Salt is good: but if the salt have lost his savor, wherewith shall it be seasoned? It is neither fit for the land, nor fit for the dunghill; but men cast it out. He that hath ears to hear let him hear."

WARNING: Not everyone is called to sell all that they have. That command came to me. What Jesus Christ, the Savior is asking is this: "Will you allow Me to become your all in all?" That will transpire to each individual as HE sees and calls each one to OBEDIENCE TO HIS WILL and not ours.

CHAPTER 1 Tree of Knowledge

Last night, I listened to a preacher from Singapore. He said that the first sin was the sin of self-righteousness. I perceived immediately that what the Father had shown him was a simple, yet the profound Truth that is foundational. I went to bed pondering this Truth.

The Lord woke me up early, and literally, by the Holy Spirit, began speaking this into my spirit.

What the Lord was revealing was the "king-pin", the original sin, the iniquity of our first father and mother; AND the iniquity that they passed on to each one of us. This revelation ties into what is written in this book, and the practical application for each of His Children, the "capstone". Here it is:

The Tree of the Knowledge of Good and Evil = self-righteousness = religion = being "god like", without God! Pure evil masked as light. (Babylon is that kingdom of light, which is really gross darkness.) That prince is a very bright light, but the light is a blinding light, a light that does not illuminate the darkness at all, it is self-contained.....those "mind blinding spirits".

6

Self-righteousness = filthy rags, rags filled with human blood, (works of our own hands, relying on our own good works and strength to gain access to the Most Holy God) which is a stench to man and to the true God. Jezebel, which is that "spirit of whoredoms" spoken of in Hosea 4:12..."My people ask counsel at their stocks, and their staff declareth unto them: for "the spirit of whoredoms" hath caused them to err and they have gone a whoring from under their God." That "spirit of error/the spirit of Egypt" - dead flies, sets up Baal worship. Baal means "lord", lord of the house i.e. IDOLS. There are individual idols; family idols, which have been passed down i.e. "familiar spirits", which follow families; idols in church fellowships/organized religion; and then national idols, ones in which the whole nation follows.

Whatever "god" you are following, and we ALL follow something or someone, even those who state there is no god, have actually set themselves up to be god; will determine the sacrifice because, there is a "Law of Sacrifice" set up in the spirit realm and the "god" you serve WILL dictate the sacrifice.

The Lord also spoke of what fruits self-righteousness produces: pride, and pride produces destruction -

(pride is not bowing to the Lord Jesus Christ) and that is more than just accepting Him as Savior. He needs to become your Lord-King! What HE says, you DO.

Proverbs   16:18.....Pride   goes   before destruction, and a haughty spirit before a fall.

CHAPTER 2 The Journey

Obedience is the outward evidence that you believe. You do what He says, because you believe He is truly God and you have the "fear of the Lord" working in you.

Therefore, in the world there are only two classes of individuals - Believers and unbelievers. The Lord of Hosts will still guide in unbelief (Psalm 78) because everyone has areas of unbelief that need to be dealt with via the Word through the Holy Spirit.

When you are convicted by the Holy Spirit regarding unbelief, REPENT (change your mind and agree with what the Lord is showing you), turn around and confess your sin of unbelief, apply the Blood of Jesus via repentance and accepting the price that He paid for you on the Cross for access to the Throne of God, the Father. For Jesus's Blood is the True God's blood sacrifice to wash you clean of all filthiness. Then obey His Word to start the journey out of the unbelief. Faith is the substance of things hoped for, of evidence of things not seen. Abraham's faith and obedience.

The journey is "taking the land" (putting your hand to the plow), the promise land = Your spirit, your soul (mind, will and emotions) and body. The true temple of God (Holy of Holies) = your spirit;

The Holy Place = your soul; The Outer Court = your body.

Entering into His Rest, the Rest that is spoken of in Hebrews 4, is taking Jesus' full and complete Blood Sacrifice, totally. (His spirit, soul and body sacrifice.) You would be surprised of how many of His children, deep in their beings, do not take His complete sacrifice as payment and access to the Heavenly Father. That is why in Hebrews 4 it states: "Let us therefore fear: lest a promise being left us of entering into His rest, any of you should seem to come short of it...verse 10: For he that is entered into His rest, he also hath ceased from his own works, as God did from His. Verse 11: Let us labor therefore to enter into that rest, lest any man fall after the same example of unbelief."

The journey is His Command: "Follow Me!" BUT the journey will cost you everything: death to self and flesh. But His Promise is life abundant to all who will lose their lives for His sake. Coming out of Egypt is the journey of facing your unbelief and the lies, which you have believed. You will choose to either obey or disobey His Word, whether it is His Still

Small Voice or the written Word that the Holy Spirit brings to your remembrance. The wilderness that you will enter into is the place where testings, refining, and sanctification takes place - being set apart for Him and His service. Vessels of Honor being formed into His Likeness.

He promises that He will do it through you: His strength, His comfort, His protection, His provision, His leading, His cleansing: BUT you have to continue to decide to follow Him and His direction at ALL COST!

We are all at different stages of the journey. Some are seasoned, though not yet arrived. Some are on their way, and there are those who have yet begun, but will in DUE season. This is why it is VITAL to obey the command in 2 Corinthians 10: "but measuring themselves by themselves, and comparing themselves among themselves, are not wise." If we get our eyes OFF Jesus Christ and start looking at another, we will start to compare with each other, and it will produce self-righteousness AND self-loathing. Let the Word read you; let the gentle Holy Spirit guide you out of your fears, unbelief and self-righteousness - by receiving ALL of Jesus' work on the cross. Don't continue to make mental and verbal excuses for your sin and iniquity. Face it with Jesus - He's lovingly awaiting for you.

I heard someone make this profound statement: "God is too big to be on anyone's side. WE need to choose to be on HIS SIDE!"

Like Paul wrote: Philippians 3......"I count not myself to have apprehended, but this one thing I do, forgetting those things which are behind, and reaching forth unto those things which are before. I press toward the mark for the prize of the high calling of God in Christ Jesus....Let us therefore, as many be perfect (mature), be thus minded; and in anything ye be otherwise minded, God shall reveal even this unto you.....Looking unto Jesus, the Author and Finisher of our Faith.

CHAPTER 3 Gates of Grace Closing

April 27, 2009

Gates of Grace Closing? Times of the Gentiles coming to a close? And "A Sign?"

Peter was given the assignment to bring the Gospel of the Risen Lord and Savior, Jesus Christ to the gentiles so they might be saved. Acts 10.

The gospel to the gentiles began with an Italian centurion, of the Italian Band, Cornelius and his household, who came to the saving knowledge of the New Covenant in Jesus Christ. So a man from Italy was the first gentile on the planet to receive the glorious gospel of Jesus Christ.

Here is a news article that I ran across from Italy on this date, April 27, 2009.

(ANSA) - Rome, April 27, 2009 - Italy's civil protection department has issued a bad weather alert for several Italian regions as a major storm system sweeps through the peninsula. The high winds have already claimed two victims in separate incidents in Sicily. In the first, the 63 year old custodian of a villa in Palermo was killed by a falling branch as he was closing the villa's main gate; while a second, 62 year old man was killed near Messina when the wind blew a gate he was closing off its tracks and on top of him........

The age of the two men are 63 and 62.....I wonder if there is a prophetic implication regarding the age of the gentiles and Israel.

Israel's official date of birth: 1948. 1948 + 62 = 2010; 1948 + 63 = 2011

Interestingly the great shakings of the planet began in 2010, as scientists state that the "axle of the planet" had been moved by these earthquakes and caused the earth to "wobble".

Chile: February 27, 2010

Christchurch, New Zealand: September 4, 2010

Japan: March 11, 2011

Then I came across a vision from Maurice Sklar, a Jewish Believer in Messiah Jesus Christ....

CHAPTER 4 Closing the Gates of Grace

Tonight I watched as the Holy Spirit give me a vision:

I saw two massive gate doors - both on the right and the left of the earth. They were made out of gold with precious gems embedded in them. They were positioned over the earth in the spirit realm. On the other side of the gates was heaven. On our side of the gates was the earth suspended in space. Then I saw a mighty angel on each side of the two gates. They were standing as sentries guarding the doorway or portal from the two realms. They each had a large sword in their hands that was on fire, it seemed to spin around perpetually in every direction, and it shot these flames out all around them. I was amazed and awed at their glory and size. They seemed as large as the earth below them. The gates were even larger in size than they were! Both angels and the gates were glowing as bright as the sun, it seemed. On the heavenly side – light was streaming like a river flowing toward the earth. As I looked into the glorious light, I saw the Lord sitting on His Throne in great majesty with many crowns on His head. He had an iron/bronze - looking scepter in His right hand

and an old-fashioned-looking harvesting sickle in the other.

Suddenly, I heard His Voice. It sounded like a roaring ocean of water and wind as He spoke. I have never heard such a sound before. He said:

"The time has come to close the gates of grace upon the earth. The nations have rejected Me and My Father long enough. Lift the coverings of protection off of those nations that have chosen Babylon over my Kingdom. I will no longer protect them from reaping what they have sown."

Then the two angels on each side of the golden gate leaves began to move slowly to shut the giant doorway/portal. I noticed that this was a slow process, because I saw the seasons change on the earth and some years pass before it was fully closed. As it was closing, I was able to look closer at the river of light that was pouring upon the earth. In it was every blessing and healing grace, forgiveness, unconditional agape love, and the constant flow of angels carrying all these wonderful blessings to the earth. Right before the gates shut, I heard the Voice of the Lord say: "Come up here, my Bride, and escape the wrath that is about to be poured upon the earth."

I heard a nearly deafeningly loud blast of heavenly trumpets from both those angels at the same time, and suddenly, I saw multitudes of souls - millions and millions of them - ascending out of the earth very fast in a flash of light. The river of light coming through the gates met them in the upper atmosphere of the earth and then reversed itself and all the souls and the river of light went back up out of the earth and into the closing gates back into heaven.

Then I saw the gates finish shutting completely - at a much faster rate now after the souls from earth had finished going into heaven. Then, it became so dark that I could no longer see the stars even. There was no more river of light flowing down upon the earth. The earth was covered in what looked like white neon hexagon shapes in a web above the earth (please see my teaching "Visions from the Dallas Revival 1985" on my website). It rapidly became opaque where I could no longer see the earth underneath. I just saw a brownish looking color - like a stagnant pond - where the oceans and land could be seen only a few moments before. Then, nearly just as fast, the whole earth seemed to be swallowed up in the thickest black darkness I had ever seen. It was like a black hole in the universe. It made the rest of the universe look light in comparison, if I could describe it that way.

I felt so sick and hopeless as I saw this. Then, just as I had heard back in the vision in 1985, I began hearing the screams of millions upon millions of souls that I knew were trapped in that darkness below the earth. The Holy Spirit then spoke to me and said:

"This is now coming upon the whole earth as a snare and a trap. This is what the nations have chosen. As they have done, so shall it be done to them. As they have cursed, so shall they be cursed. As they have condemned, so shall they be condemned. The time of My Wrath shall surely come. The nations shall drink of the wine of the wrath of My Cup that I have mixed for them. Woe! Woe! Woe to the earth for the hour of her judgment has surely come! Babylon shall now fall and be consumed by the fire of My Wrath."

Then I realized that these were still events to come in the future. But I also somehow knew that it was imminent. Once again, I saw the doors of the gates of grace still remained partially open. I knew that this was our present time now. I was so relieved to see the river of light flowing into the earth again. But, the doors were closing fast! They weren't fully opened as they were even a few years ago. I knew that we didn't have much more time.

The Lord spoke again so loudly and powerfully:

"WARN THEM! Time is very short! You must preach the gospel and work while it is still daylight. The night comes very soon, and no man can then harvest in the time of grace ever again. The doors of grace are beginning to close. REPENT1 REPENT11 REPENT O EARTH before the river of light stops flowing! Then you will face Me, not as Merciful Savior, but as the Judge of all the earth. Who will hear and heed the final call of the silver trumpet's clarion of Grace, Grace? My Spirit will not strive with sinful man forever. Come to Me now while there is still a little time left. I am coming soon for My Overcoming Bride. Keep your lamps burning....Watch and Pray.....I AM AT THE DOORS OF GRACE1

They are closing quickly....Come into My Ark of safety....come into the Bridal Chamber and the doors will SHUT....I AM COMING FOR YOU, MY BELOVED1"

I pray that we all take heed to God's prophetic warning and be ready when He appears for HIs Glorious, Waiting Bride.

Love in our Messiah,

Maurice Sklar

CHAPTER 5 Because they Hate

January 22, 2013

The Holy Spirit has brought back to remembrance several deep truths that He has shown me; and actual experiences with people, in His Church, which contain "a mixture"; the "dead flies" in which this book unveils. And the necessity of deep cleansing that needs to take place in the Body of Christ, so we can become that Glorious Church that our Lord and Savior, Jesus Christ is coming for in the Clouds of Glory. I don't want to be ashamed at His appearing. And Jesus cries: "When I return, will I find Faith on the earth?"

What I will share first, is what dwells in each human being, the roots of iniquity of our fathers. AND what needs to be dealt with in each one of us, who Names the Name of Christ. As the Word declares:

2 Timothy 2:19..."...The Lord knows them that are his. And, Let everyone that names the name of Christ depart from iniquity."

The "spirit of self-hatred" is a stronghold. The more a person has self-hatred, the more dangerous they are to themselves AND to others, and to the Lord and His Kingdom.

Remember the command of Jesus? Mark 12: 30,31...."And you shall love the Lord your God with all your heart, and with all your soul, and with all your mind, and with all your strength. The second is this, "You shall love your neighbor as yourself. There is no other commandment greater than these."

Self-hatred is actually a form of self-righteousness, which is a stench. "For our righteousness is as filthy (bloody) rags." Isaiah 64:6. It is a mirror of the Prince of Darkness, and his character! This spirit dwells in the "flesh" realm of each of us, and needs to be put to death via "taking up our cross and following the Lord Jesus Christ, by the Holy Spirit, daily."

The "spirit of hatred" is an iniquitous spirit passed down through the ages from our first father and mother, in the Garden. And when we look through the eyes of "self-hatred" towards God, towards ourselves, and towards each other, we can't walk in the love of the Father, and it will affect our very walk with Him, and how we "appear" to the lost and dying world that Jesus, in His Perfect Love, became the Sacrifice. This MUST be confronted in each of us as believers, because the "end of the commandment" is charity (or Love) our of a pure heart. 1 Timothy 1:5..."Now the end of the commandment is charity out of a pure heart, and of a good conscience, and of faith unfeigned."

CHAPTER 6 Envy – A Deadly Spirit

NOTE: Complete forgiveness and blessing and deep prayer, have gone forth for the individuals in the examples I will share. Also, allowing the Holy Spirit to deal with me in the deepest levels of my heart to be cleansed, too.

Envy = Evil = and lust is the tap root (James 3:16..For where envying and strife is, there is confusion and every evil work). The Greek word for strife in this verse, means: a desire to put one's self forward: and in this verse confusion = Babel....i.e. Babylon -man's religion.

Satan was filled with pride when he started looking at himself instead of the Lord God. Then he started lusting for the worship that The Most High God deserved and the Lord's Glory. The lust birthed envy. NOW ---that spirit of envy lusts after Satan's "false glory" i.e. riches, power, men's honor, ------the Babylon system (the evil eye) Matthew 6:22.."The light of the body is the eye: if therefore thine eye be single, thy whole body shall be full of light.. 23: BUT if thine eye be evil, thy whole body shall be full of darkness. If therefore the light that is in thee be darkness, how great is that darkness! 24.

No man can serve two masters: for either he will hate the one, and love the other; or else he will hold to the one, and despise the other. Ye cannot serve God and mammon". I Timothy 6:10...For the love of money is the root of all evil: which while some coveted after, they have erred from the faith, and pierced themselves through with many sorrows."

The answer to envy...is deep, deep, true repentance from the heart; Matthew 6:33..." But seek ye first the kingdom of God, and His righteousness; and all these things shall be added unto you."

That is why the Lord WARNS us NOT to show Babylon (anyone with the spirit's of lust and envy operating in them, your possessions, including the "precious pearls" of truth and revelation that the Lord has opened up to you) or they (Babylon will take your possessions , and trample your pearls and rend you deeply) , for their own- greedy of gain = the wolf spirit.)

Isaiah's word to Hezekiah: Isaiah: 39.

In James 4:5...."Do ye think that the scripture saith in vain, The spirit that dwells in us, lusts to envy?" The spirit of lust that every person was born with is the womb or harlot that entices a person to sin, which in the end brings death. James 1:15: "Then when lust hath conceived, it brings forth sin, and sin, when it is finished, brings forth death."

When lust is untamed, it turns into the beast of lasciviousness......unbridled lust; pleasure at any and all cost. Which we are just beginning to see in this generation.

Lust unlocks the door to that deadly spirit----envy. Envy wraps around our "bowels" of emotions. Envy will cause death. It was the spirit of envy in the religious leaders that betrayed our Lord Jesus to the Cross. Pilot stated that he knew that it was because of envy that the Scribes and Pharisees delivered up Jesus for death .(Matthew 27:18} Proverbs 27:4 states: Wrath is cruel, and anger is outrageous, BUT who is able to stand before envy? " Not even Jesus Christ could stand before that spirit of envy. Jesus, in His earthly ministry, could only stand before the religious leaders of the temple for an "ordained" short time. He then had to actually go into hiding for his physical safety. (Matthew 12:14, 15, 16)

Envy is the black spirit that is masked, sometimes as hatred. Envy is not jealousy, which can be a holy emotion. The Word states" "I AM a jealous God." Envy has destroyed many relationships in the family. Cain envied

Able and killed him. Esau envied Jacob, and wanted to kill him; Joseph's brothers were more than jealous, they envied Joseph's anointing and favor and also wanted to kill him.

Below is a personal experience that I have had to deal with all my life. It has only been in the last 27 years, since the Holy Spirit started giving revelation of what the true battle was, behind the scenes, in the spirit realm. God's Word is true, and what He states is true and it will take place sometime in this walk of following the Savior. And that is: Matthew 10:34-36..."Think not that I am come to send peace on earth: I came not to send peace, but a sword. For I am come to set a man at variance against his father, and the daughter against her mother, and the daughter in law against her mother in law.

And a man's foes shall be they of his own household." The relationships that Jesus named aren't all inclusive, He is making a point, that the Heavenly Father has NO GRANDCHILDREN in heaven.

Every single person must decide for himself or herself that Jesus died and rose again for them.

If you are the only one in your household, following the Lord Jesus Christ, you are a light, and often times, salt, which can sting when there is spiritual infection in the house. Pray, forgive, remit your family's sins and iniquities. You are the priest that can stand before the Throne and apply the Blood of Jesus for your family through repentance, that your house may be saved. (Even those that "say" they know Jesus Christ, but in "works" deny Him.) Titus 1:16....They profess that they know God; but in works they deny Him being abominable, and disobedient, and unto every good work reprobate."

My Story: AND a SERIOUS WARNING to any that "Honors the Lord with their lips, but their heart is far from Him." REPENT.

Personally, I have felt and seen that spirit (a devouring spirit) in one of my own relatives' eyes. On one occasion, on the phone, I literally felt a black claw reach through the phone, by word's spoken and tone of voice, and that spirit scratched my spirit. I lost my peace. Only when I went to bed that night, the Holy Spirit moved on my own spirit and I had my peace back again. Again, the Holy Spirit spoke that verse: ".........But who is able to stand before envy?

I have taken The Lord's warning very seriously regarding this relative. Before, what I saw in her face was anger and bitterness. Now, I see a spirit in her eyes, which wants to literally destroy me. The Holy Spirit always warned me to "walk cautiously with her". He always warned of treachery from her. Now, since she made some kind of choice in her spirit, the Lord says: "DEADLY". He has promised me:" Complete severing of the relationship."

Pride (not humble before the Lord due to lies and offenses in the heart against the Lord) the person is filled with lust which results to envy which results in death.

Envy occurs when a person lacks another's superior quality, achievement, or possession and either desires it or wishes that the other lacked it. At the core of envy seems to be an upward social comparison that threatens a person's self-esteem: another person has something that the envier considers to be important to have. If the other person is perceived to be similar as the envier, the aroused envy will be particularly intense, because it signals to the envier that it just as well could have been him or her who had the desired object.

In some cultures, envy is often associated with the color, green, as in "green with envy". The phrase "green-eyed monster" refers to an individual whose current actions appear motivated by envy. This is based on a line from Shakespeare's Othello.

Envy in religion:

Envy is one of the seven deadly sins, and is specifically mentioned in the Book of Proverbs. It is considered sinful because envious people ignore their own blessings, and focus on others' status rather than their own spiritual growth. In the New Testament, envy is the clear cause of Jesus' crucifixion.

Envy is often confused with the Deadly Sin of covetousness, or greed, a desire for material wealth (which may or may not belong to others).

Envy in Behavior:

Hatred is often envy in disguise. Envy knows no gratitude. Envy cannot be pacified. These statements describe a few of Envy's "traits".

Envy is characterized by the Machiavellian machinations of the internally weak, self-loathing, unduly proud and peasant minded. Enviers cross all social, economic, educational and professional boundaries. Envy is found among the greats in history, laborers, elite, siblings, co-workers, "friends", individuals, academia, groups, peoples and nations.

Biblical examples demonstrate Envy's deceptive, merciless, and malignant personality. Centuries later, secular scholars and philosophers (e.g., Aristotle and Plato) discovered Envy's true nature the will to completely destroy the envied. Due to Envy's deeply deceptive nature, too often the envied is unaware of being envied; and so, are at a genuine loss as to why a person or group would vent "inexplicable" cruelty on them. Exacerbating matters, the cruelty is regularly denied directly and indirectly by the envier. This renders witnesses to the envy dynamic ignorant to the truth as well.

Enviers often seize the very questioning of their actions to malign the envied; thereby laying the foundation for wider, subtle and blatant, misrepresentation, accusation, and attacks upon the reasoning faculties and character of the envied. The envier's intent is always to destroy the envied, to the envier's comfort and delight, since the envied inadvertently aggravates the envier's deepest inferiority feelings.

31

Tragically, the envied who doesn't realize Envy's nature, or that they are being envied (most don't) is at huge risk for permanent loss and devastation since envy is parent to history's greatest atrocities and scapegoating.

Examples: Jesus Christ, Joan of Arc, Martin Luther King,(Holocaust-Hitler wanted to be an artist, and "envied" some of the Jewish Artists.)

Biblical Example

General references: (Job 5:2,3; Psalms 37:1,7;49:16;73:3,17-20;112:10) Cain, of Abel (Genesis 4:4-8) [Murder] Philistines, of Isaac (Genesis 26:14) [Theft, resentment] Leah, of Rachel (Genesis 30:15) [Hatred, resentment, competition] Laban's sons, of Jacob (Genesis 31:1) [Hatred of success] Joseph's brethren, Joseph (Genesis 37:4-11,19,20; Acts 7:9) [Envies favor, will to murder, lie, sabotage success, destroy innocent] Miriam and Aaron, of Moses (Numbers 12:1-10) [Pride, accusation] Korah, Dathan, and Abiram, of Moses (Numbers 16:3; Psalms 106:16-18) [Wide slandering, criticism, fomenting hostilities based on falsehoods, recruiting others against the envied] King Saul, of King David (1 Samuel 18:8,9,29;20:31) [Ingratitude, hatred, murder] Haman of Mordecai (Esther 5:13) [Wholesale slander, fomenting violence and hatred to envied's destruction] The princes of Babylon, of Daniel (Daniel 6:4) [Attempts to destroy professionally, personally, by plot, undermining, sabotage, and deception]

Envy and a sense of injustice

There is a possibility and/or theory that states of envy can mutate into a sense of concern for maintaining justice; though this is assumed to be for a sense of justice that only surrounds ones self. There is no evidence of such a sense of injustice being for the concern of others, but no proof of it not being so either since this is a mutated emotion we are talking about. It is often said by the individuals that are envious of another (particularly children) "That's not fair!" when someone else has something that they wish they could have. Curiously, people do not tend to think of justice to the other being of priority but instead only think of the fact that the other person is being selfish as priority (such priority in it's self could be thought of unjust).

CHAPTER 7 The Wolf Spirit

The Lord of Hosts has uncovered, in part, what a wolf spirit is: Again, it was through an actual experience I had with the relative that is walking in envy towards me.

In August of 2005, I had a dream about a wolf that had it's back legs tied with twine. The wolf was part of my family. I reached down and took the twine off it's back legs. It then had the freedom to run fully. It ran and stood between two sheep. When I awoke from the dream, I asked the Lord what it meant. He was giving me a warning of what was about to take place that day, at lunch. He gave me a second warning on the way to meet the envious relative and a Jewish friend of hers that had accepted Jesus as his Messiah.

Well, at lunch, the Jewish friend and I were "really connecting in the Holy Spirit". There was a very important Word the the Lord of Hosts wanted to get across to him (regarding bitterness and the Holocaust). I began to be transparent with the Jewish man, giving my own example of what iniquity I had fallen into because of the anti-christ spirit, masked in a person claiming to "know" Jesus. Right in the middle of my story, the relative interrupted and began to share a story about me. What she shared was the most humiliating thing she knew about me. (NOTE: My mother shared what I had done and even fabricated some of the facts.) After she finished the story I thought to myself: "So this is how a "wolf spirit" operates." I did not feel any anger towards her, nor did I experience ANY shame for this past sin of mine. But on my way home, the Holy Spirit said that there would be a severing of the relationship, by HIS HAND. AND that her voice will be silenced."

This past Spring, 2006. I had another dream about me battling wolves. What I found out was that this same relative's ex-husband, was sharing the same humiliating story that I mentioned above, with his relatives, and with fabricated facts.

Through prayer, with a very precious prayer partner, the Lord revealed that when the wolves are (howling), they are talking about someone and their past sins... SINS.....THAT HAVE BEEN PLACED UNDER THE PRECIOUS BLOOD OF JESUS, THROUGH THE PERSON'S REPENTANCE.

The wolf spirit is actually an anti-christ spirit.

The Lord shared that a person who is speaking against a believer, in gossip/slander, is actually trampling the Blood of Jesus under foot. Wow, no wonder the sin of the tongue is deadly.......As it is written, "Speak evil of NO MAN." And no wonder the Body of Christ is so crippled. We are biting and devouring one another, like "eating our own flesh" as we are all one body. (Those who are truly in Jesus Christ).

Being delivered out of Egypt and Egypt out of us. (Dead flies in the ointment)

Ezekiel 29:15,16....speaking of Egypt's judgment: " It (Egypt) shall be the basest of the kingdoms; neither shall it exalt itself any more above the nations: for I will diminish them, that they shall no more rule over the nations." 16...."And it shall be no more the confidence of the house of Israel, which brings their iniquity to remembrance, when they shall look after them; but they shall know that I am the Lord God. Egypt is the "spirit of whoredoms" which causes err, and have gone a whoring from under their God.." (a spirit of dizziness)

Hosea 4:12 and Ezekiel 23:27.."Thus will I make thy lewdness to cease from thee, and thy whoredom brought from the land of Egypt."

Father forgive me and my brothers and sisters. We have so little time and it is time to wake up and cleanse ourselves from all filthiness of the flesh and spirit, for truly the COMING OF THE LORD IS NIGH, EVEN AT THE DOOR.

CHAPTER 8 Ritualistic Sacrifice of Porneia

The "spirit of porneia" (fornication = whoredoms in English) and the root word of today's pornography - is greater than just "looking" at perverse photos. This spirit and kingdom are described in

Revelation 2.

Father showed that this "spirit" is the one that sets up "ritualistic sacrifice', the sacrifice which I spoke of on page 3; it is actually a religious spirit. This spirit "rapes", and again it is more than just a sexual reference. It truly is the "spirit of violence" which the Word speaks; it is a "religious and death spirit". Our promise and Word regarding warfare against this prince: "Violence shall no more be heard in thy land, nor wasting nor destruction within thy borders; but thou shalt call thy walls Salvation, and thy gates Praise," Isaiah 60:18.

Here is another example of "dead flies in the ointment" (anointing) of a believer, a leader, bound by this spirit of iniquity - devils.

Back in January 1988, a famous evangelist from Louisiana had been uncovered. He had been going to New Orleans and hiring prostitutes. When a reporter uncovered his sin, nationally, he wept openly before his congregation and asked for forgiveness. He later shared that he had a bondage with pornography (a spirit of destruction) since early childhood. His wife also had a dream about the "monster spirit" that had entered into their bedroom and just tore everything up and turned all the furniture over. When his wife awoke, she asked: "Is this what we are fighting?"

The Holy Spirit spoke to me during this and said: "It's PRIDE that he needs to confess and repent. The Lord was showing that Pride was the tap root of iniquity, meaning what gave its power and the legal ground in him and his family to "steal, kill, and destroy".

His denomination wanted to give him "time-off" from the pulpit, and counsel him through this period. BUT he would not bow to their authority in his life and left that denomination and opened up his own ministry. He went along, looking like all was well, UNTIL, another episode in California, other prostitutes were uncovered, again. The bondage was still alive and strong in his life.

The spirit of perversion feeds on pride. One of the great deceptions that turned Sodom into such perversion was pride. Ezekiel 16:49-50..."Behold, this was the iniquity of thy sister Sodom, PRIDE, fullness of bread, and abundance of idleness was in her and in her daughters, neither did she strengthen the hand of the poor and needy. And they were haughty, and committed abomination before Me: therefore I took them away as I saw good."

Isn't it interesting that the homosexual community calls it "gay pride" They have deeply wounded spirits and are very deceived. An illegal touch is all it takes for the kingdom of darkness to plant his evil seed in a child, and set up Satan's domain in a child's heart. It can lie dormant for years, until a situation touches that childhood pain, and then the fruit manifests. We are seeing countless men and women, even young children, "forsaking" the natural law of their own bodies. We are living in desperate times, where the Love and Light of Jesus Christ needs to manifest in His people. BUT OUT OF A HEART OF HIS LOVE FOR THE PERSON. For His Love will draw them into Truth.

I heard a statement about pride. There is no pride in the Beloved. What did the Heavenly Father openly say about His son when He spoke audibly? "This is my beloved Son, of Whom I am well pleased." The Father

40

never mentioned: "I'm proud of you."
Interesting observation.

CHAPTER 9 Principles of This Depth of Warfare

The most important truth to remember when you 'put your hand to the plow", and begin through the Holy Spirit with the Word of God, to confront the "evil-Baal's" in your own heart, is the power of the Blood of Jesus. When applied via repentance, His Blood speaks for us at His Throne, and will silence the "avenger of blood". His Blood is the life giving force for our cleansing and deliverance, and protection. And you apply it by repentance and remitting sins.

The second most important truth in this level of warfare is DO NOT FEAR the "gods" (demons) that you are facing. Fear is sin and is rooted in unbelief. Throughout the Word, He commands us not to fear: 2 Kings 17:36, 39..."But the Lord, who brought you up out of the land of Egypt with great power and a stretched out arm, Him shall ye fear, and Him shall ye worship, and to Him shall ye do sacrifice. But the Lord your God ye shall fear: and He shall deliver you out of the hand of all your enemies."

1 John 4:4..."Ye are of God, little children, and have overcome them: because greater is

He that is in you, than he that is in the world." And: "For God has not given you a spirit of fear, but of power, of love, and of a sound mind." 2 Timothy 1:7

The third important command is: "Watch what you speak." Exodus 23:13 "And in all things that I have said unto you be circumspect: and make no mention of the name of other gods, neither let it be heard out of thy mouth." Exodus 22:28 "Thou shalt not revile the gods, nor curse the ruler of thy people."

This command is vital for you, your children, and your family's protection. What this is speaking of is, don't use the ancient names of the gods when you speak; the names given to the "gods" of the nations in the Torah. Speak of the "spirit's fruit", or how it manifests; example: death, pride, envy, deception, witchcraft, lasciviousness (unbridled lust), and blasphemy. Remember that you have been given authority:

Luke 10:19 "Behold I give unto you power (authority) to tread on serpents and scorpions, and over all the power of the enemy; and nothing shall by any means hurt you."

CHAPTER 10 Two Giants In the Land

January 24, 2013

There are two giants in each of us that we, by the Blood of the Lamb and the Word of our testimony MUST defeat, they are: fear and murmuring, which is found in an evil heart of unbelief.

"Death and Life are in the power of the tongue; and they that love it shall eat the fruit thereof." Proverbs 18:21. James gives a very severe warning about the tongue. James 3…..The tongue sets on coarse nature (things in motion) and the fires of hell (demons) set it. The enemy always wants to get a hold of the tongue due to the spiritual power that is in it.

Deuteronomy 30:14, 15, 19 - "But the word is very nigh unto thee, in thy mouth, and in thy heart, that thou mayest do it…See, I have set before thee this day life and good, and death and evil:….19: I call heaven and earth to record this day against you, that I have set before you life and death, blessing and cursing: therefore choose life, that both thou and thy seed may live:

THE PROPHETIC DREAM: DECEMBER 1990 FORT PAYNE, ALABAMA

The dream started with my four year old son and I about to climb a hill. We passed a car that was on "fire", and I saw a blond hair man in the back seat. I knew that he had started the fire, AND I knew we needed to get out of the way, because the car was going to explode.

I took my son's hand and began running up the forested hill. I then HEARD and FELT the explosion of the car. We continued up the hill to a "warehouse" looking building. I opened the door and saw all manner of demonic articles, evil looking stuff, and I immediately closed the door as to NOT go in there. I woke up.

It was really early in the morning, and I was pondering the powerful dream, the phone rang, and on the other end was a prayer partner from Huntsville, AL....she was sobbing and said: "Kevin is dead!" I knew immediately that the dream was about him. I asked what happened.

She told me that he stopped by a few weeks ago and said he felt really strange. Then the night of the dream, his death...He was in a graveyard with a woman, and he got out of the car to "relieve himself". He started to slip and

45

grabbed a hold of a grave stone, and it fell on him and crushed him to death.

The Lord was showing me the "power of our words" from that dream. Kevin had set in motion death by his words.

February 15, 2013

Words start in the "mind". There have been many books written about the "battlefield of the mind", and the process it takes. Everything begins as a thought and then a word, and then action!

A process that takes place in the "spirit of the mind". Here it is:

Psalm 7:14..."He travaileth with iniquity, and conceived mischief, and brought forth (birthed) falsehood."

It is imperative to take captive and judge EVERY thought that comes through your mind. Part of the Armor of God is the Helmet of Salvation. Ephesians 6.

Job 15 states: "Thy mouth utters thine iniquity, and thou choosest the tongue of the crafty." This gives the process of how falsehood is born. When a person "travails" with iniquity, they are constantly rolling over in their minds lies that they believe. If a person doesn't stop the thoughts and replace the lying

46

thoughts with Truth, then mischief is conceived (an acting out of what they are believing). And it gives birth to falsehood. Which is extremely dangerous in the realm of the spirit. Self-deception.

The Holy Spirit then brought back the Word regarding: Matthew 7:21-23..."Not everyone that saith unto me, Lord, Lord, shall enter into the kingdom of heaven; but he that doth the will of my Father which is in heaven. Many will say to me in that day, Lord, lord, have we not prophesied in Thy Name? and in Thy Name have cast out devils? And in Thy Name done many wonderful works? And then I will profess unto them, I never knew you; depart from me, ye that work iniquity.

KNOWING HIM is the Salvation! He IS! And the knowledge is NOT A HEAD KNOWLEDGE - it is the heart knowledge of experience by believing and obeying Him.

Chapter 11 Taking Thoughts and the Tongue Captive

March 3, 2013

People who are continually sick - speak sickness all the time! Those are the ones, because of wounds, embrace the "spirit of infirmity" for their identity. They are believing the "lie" that if they don't always have something wrong with them, no one will love or care for them. They are operating out of an "orphan spirit", not one of "adoption by the Heavenly Father, through Jesus Christ His Son".

Jesus uncovered this type of "mask" that some people hide behind. They "really, down deep in their heart, don't want healing. John 5:5, 6, 7....."And a certain man was there, which had an infirmity 38 years. When Jesus saw him lie, and knew that he had been now a long time in that case, He saith unto him, Wilt thou be made whole? The impotent man answered him........(with excuses as to why he was still in that place of sickness and disease.)........John 5:14...Afterward Jesus found him in the temple, and said unto him, Behold, thou art made whole; sin no more, lest a worse thing come unto thee."

Taking every thought captive by "judging" the thoughts that enter the mind is vital in overcoming the enemy. If we do not do this on a moment to moment basis, the strongholds that have held us captive will never be taken down. Then a time comes, when the Lord, in His mercy and Holiness, must allow judgment in a person's life. Because of continually "choosing" death and cursing, the Lord MUST honor their free will/choice and He will "give them over" to that spirit they continually embrace and rebel against the Knowledge of the Lord and HIs Word.

NOTE: When I was living in Lyons, CO, I began having evil thoughts about an unruly neighbor boy. When these "thoughts" would enter, I immediately starting repenting and thinking that I was a horrible person for having these thoughts. It was then, the Holy Spirit "yelled" inside me: "They're NOT your thoughts!!!!!" From that "Rhema Word, He taught me about "the voice of the accuser of the brethren" and the voice of the enemy of our souls. And WHY in His Word declares: 2 Corinthians 10:4, 5, 6...

"For the weapons of our warfare are not carnal, but mighty through God to the pulling down of strong holds; Casting down imaginations, and every high thing that exalts itself against the knowledge of God, and bringing into captivity every thought to the obedience of Christ; And having in a readiness to revenge all disobedience, when your obedience is fulfilled."

The Lord in His Word gives us this promise: 1 Corinthians 11:31, 32..."For if we would judge ourselves, we should not be judged. But when we are judged, we are chastened of the Lord, that we should not be condemned with the world." Proverbs 16:6..."By mercy and truth iniquity is purged: and by the fear of the Lord men depart from evil."

Mercy, because the Lord of Hosts knows if that person is allowed to continue in those "vain imaginations" without correction, utter destruction will eventually take place, and possibly to the point of "denying the Lord Jesus Christ" and be lost for eternity. Jeremiah 10:24 .."O Lord, correct me, but with judgment; not in thine anger, lest thou bring me to nothing."

OFFENSES AND LIES WHICH CAN LEAD TO ETERNAL DAMNATION: HELL

Matthew 27:3-5.....

"Then Judas, which had betrayed Him, when he saw that He was condemned, repented himself, and brought again the thirty pieces to the chief priests and elders, saying, I have sinned in that I have betrayed the innocent blood. And they said, What is that to us. See though to that. And he cast down the pieces of silver in the temple, and departed, and went and hanged himself."

In this part of scripture, we see that Judas' understanding opens up. Judas realizes that the thoughts and imaginations of who Jesus was, were all wrong. He, Judas, had believed the lies that Satan had been telling him. But it was too late. The offenses in Judas' heart had brought him to the gate of hell. Judas made choices from this deception. And then he crossed the line in which there was no more mercy or grace for forgiveness. He was going to reap an eternal punishment due to his continual choices not to take the Lord Jesus at His Word.

Making up a "god" which resembles the true Lord only "in part", in our own imaginations can lead us into great deception, and eventually lead us to eternal damnation. We can't pick and choose what scripture to believe. The Word is Truth. And in HIs Word, The Lord of Hosts explains and says exactly Who He is. And He gives detailed "history" in His Word as to the consequences of NOT taking Him at His Word via believing thus obeying. We have to take God completely at His Word when He describes Who He is.

His desire is for "not one to perish", but in His lovingkindness, He has created us with a free will, that is cherished.

Jesus warned us over and over again, particularly in the end of times, "Don't be deceived." For if possible, the very elect would be deceived." Matthew 24:24. We must not look or FOLLOW signs and wonders, or charismatic personalities, no matter how gifted they appear. We MUST keep our entire focus on Jesus Christ and His Word, being very sensitive to the Holy Spirit and His leading. He has promised those who are truth lovers, that: "If you continue in My word, ye shall know the truth, and the truth shall MAKE you free." John 8:32.

Again, your focus must be on Jesus Christ and Him alone; not on a teacher, pastor, evangelist, prophet, or apostle. When you hear a teaching, go back and study that word with your bible; check it out yourself, at home, alone with the Word and the Holy Spirit. He is faithful, and if there is deception or a mixture; i.e. some truth, and some deception, He will unveil it. Then He will teach you to "glean".

Receiving the truth and rejecting the deception. "Study to show thyself approved unto God, a workman that needs not to be ashamed, rightly dividing the Word of Truth." 2 Timothy 2:15

CHAPTER 12 Why the Church Is Not Walking in The Power of the Lord of Hosts

Ecclesiastes 3:15..."That which hath been is now; and that which is to be hath already been; and God require that which is past."

The end times speak of Elijah having to come first. The spirit of Elijah came through John the Baptist, to prepare the way of the Lord, by calling people to repentance. Malachi 4:5 "Behold, I will send you Elijah the prophet before the coming of the great and dreadful day of the Lord....."

Elijah is a "type" of an overcomer. Elijah had to fight the prophets of Baal and the great "whore", Jezebel, that mistress of witchcrafts. 2 Kings 9:22; Nahum 3:4... "Because of the multitude of the whoredoms of the well-favored harlot, the mistress of witchcrafts." Which in reality IS the spirit of the carnal mind in each of us!........That is why He declares: "And be not conformed to this world; but be ye transformed by the renewing of your mind, that ye may prove what is that good, and acceptable, and perfect, will of God." Romans 12:2.

The reason the Body of Christ, His Church, is not walking in the power of the early Church, is because we, individually, have not divorced the "Baals" which are in our hearts and minds, i.e. "heart idols".

The Lord commands us to: "Wherefore come out from among them, and be ye separate, saith the Lord, and touch not the unclean thing; and I will receive you." 2 Corinthians 6:17. Also in His Word: "Having therefore these promises, dearly beloved, let us cleanse ourselves from all filthiness of the flesh and spirit, perfecting holiness in the fear of God." 2 Corinthians 7:1. We must have our hearts and minds pure before Him; then we will be able to walk in the full authority, in His fullness.

The "manifestation of the sons of God "(those in HIs likeness and character) , which now the creation groans for, (Romans 8:19).... will be on the earth to bring forth His Glory to all nations and prepare them for His Second Coming in the clouds of His Glory.

The Church, i.e. The Body of Christ MUST be purified from idols, which are in the deepest part of their being. The "High Places in the Heart of His People."

CHAPTER 13 High Places in the Heart of People

2 Chronicles 21:32, 33..."....and he walked in the way of Asa his father, and departed not from it, doing that which was right in the sight of the Lord. Howbeit the high places were not taken away: for as yet the people had not prepared their hearts unto the God of their fathers." The high places spoken in this scripture are the pagan shrines for worship in ancient times.

September 5, 2002 6:44 a.m.

The Lord has shown me this truth about the heart. At the point in our spirit i.e. heart, where we are the most deeply offended at the Lord, is where the veil of the Spirit is and the veil of the flesh. An individual makes the decision to either go through into the Holy of Holies (the person's own heart) where the Holy Spirit dwells, to continue to trust Him fully by following Him (obedience) OR the person decides the cost is too great and returns to the flesh where "religion" dwells. Instead of turning their hearts toward the Lord, allowing the Holy Spirit to surface the darkness and filth in their hearts, people get religious. Then they are given over to the works of their own hands (idols they trust in)....things start to turn upside down in their lives...and then they "shake their fists and say, Why God did You allow this to happen?" They are self-deceived and then they rage against the Lord of Hosts.

Job 15:5, 12, 13...."Why doth thine heart carry thee away? and what do thy eyes wink at, that thou turns thy spirit against God, and let such words go out of thy mouth?' As it is written in

James 1:22...."But be ye doers of the Word, and not hearers only, deceiving your own selves." (Laodicea Church)

September 8, 2002 3:42 a.m.

The Lord showed me how "religion" is set up in a person's heart. Unbelief and lies.

There is an offense that takes place in childhood. The child prayed and their prayer went, at least to their understanding, unanswered. They were abused, neglected, abandoned, or had deep disappointment in their lives. Violence filled their home, verbal and/or physical. Something happens to the child. They are hurt. Satan takes this opportunity to sow seeds of destruction, through lies about the character of God. The child believes the lies that Jesus did this to him.

Now the child cannot turn to the True Lord, because the child believed the lie. We are created to worship. And we will worship someone or something.

Then since the child believes the lie, deep within the child's spirit, they turn from the Only True God. With this heart decision, Satan is now legally allowed to set up the "spirit of whoredoms" in the child's heart. This is an actual demonic power. An Egypt spirit...dead flies...This spirit will cause error.

Hosea 4:10, 11, 12..."because they have left off to take heed to the Lord. Whoredom and wine and new wine take away the heart. My people ask counsel at their stocks, and their staff (what a person trusts and leans on) declareth unto them: for the spirit of whoredoms hath caused them to err, and they have gone a whoring from under their God. The anti-christ spirit is unleashed to set up a "form of godliness"-religion (the Mystery Babylon spirit spoken of in Revelation), instead of a relationship with the Lord of Hosts. Then the "light" that is in them becomes great darkness. As it is written in

2 Timothy 3:5, 6, 7..."Having a form of godliness but denying the power thereof; from such turn away. For of this sort are they which

creep into houses, and lead captive, silly women laden with sins, led away with divers lusts. Ever learning and never able to come to the knowledge of the truth."

That spirit of anti-christ comes out of the black, bitter nation of Babylon; the roots of deep hatred towards the living God, with an evil heart of unbelief. That is why it is written: 1 Timothy 2:8.."Lifting up holy hands without wrath and doubting."

BABYLON SYSTEM = MAMMON SPIRIT (LOVE OF MONEY)

The root of the Babylon system is "the love of money". Mammon is that spirit that operates this system. Remember what Timothy warned: 1 Timothy 6:10..."For the love of money is the root of all evil; which while some coveted after, they have erred from the faith, and pierced themselves through with many sorrows."

If a person does not worship the true and living God, by walking in His Truth, doing the Word - to obtain the blessings of obedience, then there must be a counterfeit "god to bless" the disobedient man. This counterfeit god is the god of mammon, the filthy lucre, which Timothy speaks about. NOTE: This does not say that having money is evil...it states the

LOVE OF MONEY is what is evil. It has to do with the heart of the person coveting after money - an idol.

Jesus spoke of only TWO MASTERS on this earth; one being God and one being mammon.

Matthew 6:21-24 "For where your treasure is, there will your heart be also. The light of the body is the eye. If therefore thine eye be single, thy whole body shall be full of light.

But if thine eye be evil, thy whole body shall be full of darkness. If therefore the light that is in thee be darkness, how great is that darkness. NO MAN CAN SERVE TWO MASTERS; for either he will hate the one, and love the other; or else he will hold to the one, and despise the other. Ye cannot serve God and mammon. But seek ye first the Kingdom of God and His Righteousness, and all these things shall be added unto you." Matthew 6:33.

His people must come to full repentance and allow the Holy Spirit to go deep within and uncover what "Master" they are really following.

There are more following the "mammon spirit/master" in His Body, than you can ever imagine. In this 27 year "walk on the water", following the Lamb whithersoever He goes, has uncovered this in many of His people. I have witnessed the "Lord, overturning the money changer tables" in a number of congregations across this country. And sadly, He has had to "remove" the candlestick of their fellowship because the leaders would not come to repentance. And then Jesus gets blamed for it, because we carry His Name. And yet, more wounds for His Body.

CHAPTER 14 Abomination of Desolation Spirit of Sacrifice

The abomination that causes desolation, standing in the Holy Place, is that "spirit of sacrifice" - human sacrifice, in His people. As it is written in 1 Corinthians 10:20-21..."But I say, that the things which the Gentiles sacrifice, they sacrifice to devils, and not to God: and I would not that ye should have fellowship with devils. Ye cannot drink the cup of the Lord, and the cup of devils; ye cannot be partakers of the Lord's table, and of the table of devils."

It goes back to the revelation - if you don't accept the complete sacrifice of the Blood of Jesus and His work done on the cross - all other sacrifice to "get right" with the Father is an abomination to Him because He has PAID THE ENTIRE PRICE.

The sacrifices come from an evil heart of unbelief - the heart which has set up idolatry. There is a "spiritual law" that is set in the earth: where there is another "god", there must be a sacrifice; i.e. RELIGION. That religion can be actual satanism or pharisaism (religion, set up in the Body of Christ, in the Holy of Holies, their own hearts. It's all the same "spirit").

The abortions have taken the place of the cultic Baal worship, child sacrifice. But it's not just physically killing the children that this "spirit of sacrifice" manifests itself. It is any sacrifice that has been made out of trying to get in the Lord's favor - other than the Blood of Jesus, through simple obedience to what He has told you to do; whether through His Word, or the Still Small Voice.

When the Lord roots out all the fears in a person, witchcraft loses its power of control because fear feeds the witchcraft, which is the "spirit" that opposes and is the opposite of turning to the Holy Spirit and His Word for guidance.

Jezebel (that mistress of witchcrafts) enters through fear. Trauma - fear - offensive bitterness - hate (offense towards the Lord due to NOT SEEING HIM correctly, believing lies about His Character).

The spirit of whoredoms which sets up heart idolatry, which sets up the spirit of error, which in turn, because of idolatry, opens up the gates for spirits of death and destruction in a person's life, and family.

Fear is rooted out by "Perfect Love" from the Father...for it is written: "There is no fear in love; but perfect love casteth out fear:

because fear hath torment. He that fears is not made perfect in love.

1 John 4:18. When we, <u>by faith, start believing that GOD truly Loves us perfectly,</u> and He is NOT out to do us in, then the work of plucking up the fear, with all its many faces and tentacles transpires in

a person's life. Then when this takes place, and I might "warn", it is not an overnight thing because it takes place as we take up our cross and follow Him on a moment to moment basis as He peels the onion, one layer at a time; then the "voice of iniquity" is silenced, i.e. Jezebel, i.e. witchcraft!

Saul was afraid of people. "The fear of man brings a snare; but whoso puts his trust in the Lord shall be safe." Proverbs 29:25 His heart was not right towards the Lord. Saul did not fear the Lord above everything - give the Lord God the highest honor, and respect, due Him. Then Saul turned to a "self-appointed" sacrifice, which brought forth the loss of his kingdom and the Lord's presence. Then when the Lord was silent, instead of repenting, he actually seeks out a witch, a woman with a familiar spirit for guidance. Which ultimately brings death to him and his household. (The curse of death; for the wages of sin is death.) Romans 6:23.

Witchcraft has many masks, not just the obvious occult ones. Operating out of the spirit of fear uses witchcrafts - self-appointed ways to control, manipulate the situation and the people in one's sphere of influence. Nagging, silent treatment, punishment, anger, "the letter of the law which kills", being controlled by EMOTIONS rather than the Holy Spirit and His Word.

The Lord spoke to me regarding the "controlling soul - emotional spirits"- those demons that control someone, either "the host" or people near them via their emotions. He said that these spirits which dwell in a person's soul (mind, will, and emotions) are EXCEEDING WICKED SPIRITS! Very hidden, but very active IF one is ruled by their emotions, or someone else and their emotions. It's all about CONTROL!

These people have great deceptive power - and we as the Lord's Body MUST DIE TO THE FLESH, including not allowing other's emotions to rule us. We as His People, must come alive to the Holy Spirit through willing obedience in the smallest areas of our lives. Because, there is another "spiritual law" when we allow the

65

Holy Spirit to direct us in the most mundane, smallest areas of existence and that is:

"He that is faithful in that which is least is faithful also in the much: and he that is unjust in the least is unjust also in much." Luke 16:10. This law applies to everything in our lives and in His Kingdom.

He commands us: "Draw nigh to God and He will draw nigh to you. Cleanse your hands (works - man made and trusted works) ye sinners, and purify your hearts, ye double minded." James 4:8

CHAPTER 15 Set Stones of Judgment

"For the which cause I also suffer these things: nevertheless I am not ashamed; for I know Whom I have believed, and am persuaded that He is able to keep that which I have committed unto Him against that day." 2 Timothy 1:12.

"Against that day..." I had always thought "that day" to be the judgment day on the other side of eternity. No, it is the day for here and now. That day refers to the day (days) of judgment from the curse of the law that operates in a person's life. The judgments, which we enter into while on this earth.

Through repentance, which means turning and forsaking sin and iniquity (root of sin) by "being a doer of the Word, not hearer only, the thief which comes to steal, kill, and destroy, will be bound. Remember it is written in Isaiah 1:16-20: "Wash you, make you clean; put away the evil of your doings from before mine eyes; cease to do evil; Learn to do well; seek judgment, relieve the oppressed, judge the fatherless, plead for the widow. Come now, and let us reason together, saith the Lord: though your sins be as scarlet, they shall be as white as snow; though they be red like crimson, they shall be as wool.. If ye be willing and obedient, ye shall eat the good of the land: BUT if ye refuse and rebel, ye shall be devoured with the sword: for the mouth of the Lord hath spoken it."

It's all about being willing and obedient! When we obey His Word, whether it be the written logos or His Still Small Voice, it places us in a place of protection in His Spirit. By obeying, we are keeping OUR PART of the covenant.

What you have turned over to the Lord of Hosts, through prayer and allowing Him into that part of your life, He can protect and keep while the "thief" is being bound and "his goods spoiled".

Matthew 12:28-29...."But if I (Jesus) cast out devils by the Spirit of God, then the Kingdom of God (His ruler-ship) is come unto you." This means that you are obeying and doing it HIS WAY, not yours. He becomes the Boss, not you. And this is the place that He so desires each of His Children to come into...full and complete trust in Him. And obedience is that outward sign that you DO TRUST HIM COMPLETELY. The scripture goes on to say that: "Or else how can one enter into a strong man's house (the evil spirits), and spoil his goods, except he first BIND the strong man? And then he will spoil his house."

The thieves (demons) which have operated in you, your family, and family line for generations - due to the curse of disobedience in your ancestors and in you, are bound by applying the Blood of Jesus, through repentance to each particular disobedience, (as the Holy Spirit uncovers).

Psalm 122:5..."There are Set Thrones of Judgment, the thrones of the house of David." This means there are set judgments, which are set in place from the Word of God because of the curse of the law (through disobedience). If a person is walking in covenant relationship with the Lord, the Lord is able to have and give grace and mercy in those judgments, which must take place in everyone's life. Because the Word declares: "With my soul have I desired thee in the night; yea, with my spirit within me will I seek thee early; for when Thy judgments are in the earth, the inhabitants of the world will learn righteousness." Isaiah 26:9.

Jeremiah 29:22..."But if they had stood in My Counsel, and had caused my people to hear My Words, then they should have turned them from their evil way, and from the evil of their doings."

Jeremiah 10:24... "O Lord, correct me, but with judgment,; not in thine anger, lest thou bring me to nothing." Jeremiah 8:7, 11... "Yea, the stork in the heaven knows her appointed times; and the turtle and the crane and swallow observe the time of their coming; but MY PEOPLE know not the judgment of the Lord." And in verse 11..."For they have healed the hurt of the daughter of my people slightly, saying, "Peace, peace, when there is no peace."

Even after a person is saved, there are still judgments that must take place to fulfill the law. NOW, this is where a lie has crept into the Body of Christ. It has been taught that once you accept Jesus, there is no more judgment because He took our place. Jesus DID come to fulfill the Law; He became a curse for us. BUT He - Jesus - MUST BE the LORD OF OUR LIVES in order for the work of the Cross and what He paid for to operate in our lives. When we take up OUR CROSS and FOLLOW HIM, then the higher law in the Spirit realm takes over: Romans 8:2-4..."For the law of the Spirit of Life in Christ Jesus hath made me free from the law of sin and death. For what the law could not do in that it was weak through the flesh, God sending His own Son in the likeness of sinful flesh, and for sin, condemned sin in the flesh: That the righteousness of the law might be fulfilled in us, who walk NOT after the flesh, but after the Spirit." When we, as believers, walk in disobedience, the accuser of the brethren, Satan, has authority in our lives and in our family. Thus, the curse of the law is still in operation. "The letter of the law kills, but the Spirit gives life."

This Truth of Judgment in His Body is one that "many in the Body of Christ," continually, rise up against. Their understanding is darkened by deceptive teachings in the current Church today.

As I was thinking about this book, and this vital and essential truth, the Holy Spirit dropped a picture of how I could explain what He desperately wants to get across to His people regarding His Judgments.

THE PICTURE: What the Lord dropped in my spirit was the Civil War. The Civil War was WON. Washington D. C. declared through the Emancipation Proclamation: (Purpose of the War).

"And by virtue of the power and for the purpose aforesaid, I do order and declare that all persons held as slaves within said designated States and parts of States are, and henceforward shall be, FREE; and that the Executive Government of the United States, including the military and naval authorities thereof, will recognize and maintain the freedom of said persons. " 9/22/1862

Then the Lord said to ask this question: "After the war was won, were the slaves free?" Well, yes, positionally. It had become LAW. You couldn't own another person. The war had been won, declaring freedom. BUT, we know for a fact, they were not free. And especially, in the South, where such atrocities took place, into the 20th century. They were not "considered property", but they were still treated as property by their former owners, and less than human beings.

Not until, a little, tired woman, decided: "Enough is enough!" No more moving to the back of the bus! It cost her, and it cost some people, their very lives; more blood was shed to gain the freedom that was won in 1865.

TIMES AND JUDGMENTS:

A few years ago, I was in an office. And on one of the walls was a clock, a backwards clock. The numbers were backwards, i.e., where 1:00 was supposed to be, the clock read 11:00; where 12:00 should have been, it read 6:00, and so on. The Holy Spirit stirred me; I knew that the clock represented evil, but I didn't understand why. So I asked the Lord to show me why that clock was evil. And of course, in His faithfulness He answered.

Here is what He showed me regarding that backwards clock: Ecclesiastics 8:5..."Whoso keeps the commandment shall feel no evil thing; and a wise man's heart discerns both time and judgment."

In the kingdom of darkness, that perverse spirit will try and pervert the times. Remember in the scriptures it is written: Ecclesiastics 3:1..."To everything there is a season, and a time to every purpose under the heaven...

That evil "religious" spirit twists and is able to pervert the appropriate time, when a person is walking in deception or does not understand, "what time it is in the Spirit" for themselves, their family, their nation, the Church, etc.

We need understanding and wise, obedient hearts to walk in this discernment of the Holy Spirit, especially in these perilous times in which we live. In Daniel, the Word speaks of the antichrist spirit, which attempts to pervert times and seasons of the Spirit of God, through deception and unwise hearts.

And remember, Jesus in Matthew 24, a number of times, warned us: "Take heed that no man deceive you."

The other great lie i in the Body of Christ is that as Christians, we can't have devils in us. The premise of that lie is that the Holy Spirit cannot dwell in an unclean temple. But the real Truth is that we, as believers, CANNOT be cleansed until the Holy Spirit awakens us to the sin and iniquity that dwells in us. HE is the Power that cleanses us and delivers us from evil spirits.

"Dead flies cause the ointment (anointing) of the apothecary to send forth a stinking savor." Ecclesiastes 10:1. Read again Jesus' teaching about the strongman's house in Matthew 12.

We are witnessing today, devils in His Body. The many physical and psychological problems that people are having are direct results of manifesting spirits in their lives and homes.

God pleads for Israel's obedience in Psalm 81:8-12..."Hear, O my people, and I will testify unto thee: O Israel, if thou wilt hearken unto me; There shall no strange god be in thee; neither shalt thou worship any strange god. I am the Lord thy God, which brought thee out of the land of Egypt; open thy mouth wide, and I will fill it. BUT MY PEOPLE would not hearken to My voice; and Israel would none of me. So I gave them up unto their own heart's lust; and they walked in their own counsels."

In counseling a dear sister in the Lord, who was having all sorts of destruction in her life and her son's life, I shared the above truths. She asked me: "How did I get the demons in me?" I answered her this: "First, you were born with them. You inherited them through the iniquity of the father's.

In Psalm 51:5, 6,7,9,10 - David's Psalm of confession after his adultery and then murder states this: "Behold, I was shaken in iniquity; and in sin did my mother conceive me. Behold, thou desires truth in the inward parts; and in the hidden part thou shalt make me to know wisdom. Purge me with hyssop, and I shall be clean; wash me, and I shall be whiter than snow. Hide thy face from my sins, and blot out all mine iniquities. Create in me a clean heart, O God; and renew a right spirit within me."

The second thing I told her was: "When your father sexually abused you, demons entered in and then when you added your sin to sin and iniquity to iniquity, it gave open doors to the realm of the evil spirits, and they took ground in your spirit, your soul, and your body."

This truth is being played out even in young children today. All over the news, we are witnessing ancient evil spirits, manifesting in children. Children are raping, killing, stealing, and doing all manner of evil. Remember the Word states in Proverbs 20:11.."Even a child is known by his doings, whether his work be pure, and whether it be right."

The Body of Christ must come to a DEEP, DEEP, DEEP repentance: in our spirit, our soul (mind, will and emotions) and our body. Thus the temple in which the Holy Spirit dwells will be clean and fit for the Master's Use....Vessels of Honor.

This is what the Word is talking about when it states: "Cleansing the Body of all spots and blemishes." When, as a whole, the Body of Christ, turns in full repentance, the accuser of the brethren will be "cast out of heaven" completely: Thus, the curse of the law will be broken.

There was a prophecy that was spoken by a precious sister named Carol, in Boulder, CO., during the weekly women's prayer meeting. By the Spirit, she pronounced: "This is the generation that the curse will be broken."

(Mid: 1980's when given.) I didn't understand the word at that time, but it rang as TRUTH in my spirit; so I tucked it away until the Lord of Hosts brought the Light of that Word.

(Read Isaiah 59 in reference to what I just stated.)

I think one of the most sobering statements Jesus made regarding people who call Him Lord is this: Matthew 7:21-23.."Not everyone that saith unto me, Lord, Lord, shall enter into the kingdom of God.

Heaven; but he that does the will of my Father which is heaven. Many will say to Me in that day, Lord, Lord, have we not prophesied in Thy Name? and in Thy Name have cast out devils? and in Thy Name done many wonderful works? And then I will profess unto them, I NEVER KNEW YOU; depart from Me, ye that work iniquity." Matthew 25 regarding the 10 Virgins is also very sobering. (These people honor Me with their lips, but their hearts are far from Me. Jesus)

The lost world is groaning for the manifestations of the Sons of God, believers who have "paid" the price and allowed the Spirit and the Word to dig deeply into their hearts, to root out all that is offensive and unclean; so that they are ready and fit for the

Master's use in these last days; doing great exploits for the Only True and Living God; walking in His image, in His Love, in His Authority and His Power. Jesus lovingly awaits your heart's decision.

Are you willing to pay the price to get free? It begins with a heart decision and simple, yet costly, step by step obedience. Obedience, even unto death.

CHAPTER 16 Repentance Needed From His People

"IF My People, which are called by My Name, shall humble themselves, and pray, and seek My face, and turn from wicked ways: then will I hear from heaven, and will forgive their sin, and will heal their land." 2 Chronicles 7:14.

I heard a well known Pastor/Teacher speak, after 9/11. He spoke of complacency in the Body of Christ. This is what he said: "It's in the world because it is in the Church; it's in the Church because it's in the leaders." Some other Pastor commented and said: "It's not "wickedness in a leader when they fall, its weakness."

God does not have "two standards"; one for the world and one for His people. The world "looks" at the Church and says: "What's the difference between what "they-Christians" are doing and us?" And the answer from the Throne of The Most High God: "NOTHING. I can't tell them apart".

The Word that explains the above statements is this: "Dead flies cause the ointment of the apothecary to send forth a stinking savor; so doth a little folly him that is

in reputation for wisdom and honor."–
Ecclesiastes 10:1.

The fly in scriptures has been one of the
symbols of Egypt. We have been taught that
"coming out of Egypt", like the children of
Israel, is being "born again", accepting Jesus
Christ as Savior. That IS the beginning, but we
also must continue in the story of Israel coming
out of Egypt.

They brought with them, each of them, the
"spirit of Egypt"; and it took 40 years to get
Egypt "out" of them.

That "spirit of Egypt" is known in scripture
as the "spirit of whoredoms". Ezekiel
23:27.."Thus will I make thy lewdness to cease
from thee, and thy whoredom brought from
the land of Egypt; so that thou shalt not lift up
thine eyes unto them, nor remember Egypt
anymore."

Other scriptures that speak so loudly in
these times, is also in Ezekiel 14: 2-5...."And the
Word of the Lord came unto me, saying. Son
of man, these men have set up idols in their
heart, and put the stumbling block of their
iniquity before their face: should I be enquired
of at all of them? Therefore speak unto them,
and say unto them; Thus saith the Lord God -
Every man of the house of Israel that setteth up

his idols in his heart, and putteth the stumbling block of his iniquity before his face, and

cometh to the prophet; I the Lord will answer him that cometh according to the multitude of his idols - that I may take the house of Israel in their own heart, because they are all estranged from Me through their idols."

Hosea 4:6-12....He writes: "My people are destroyed for lack of knowledge, because thou hast rejected knowledge, I will also reject thee, that thou shalt be no priest to me: seeing thou hast forgotten the law of thy God, I will also forget thy children. As they were increased, so they sinned against Me: therefore will I change their glory into shame. They eat up the sin of my people, and they set their heart on their iniquity. And there shall be, like people, like priest: and I will punish them for their ways and reward them their doings. For they shall eat, and not have enough: they shall commit whoredom, and not increase: because they have left off to take heed to the Lord. Whoredom and wine and new wine take away the heart. My people ask counsel at their stocks, and their "staff" (what they are leaning on, other than the Lord and His Word) delareth unto them: for the "spirit of whoredoms" have caused them to err, and they have gone a whoring from under their God."

James 4:7..."Hereby know we the Spirit of Truth, and the spirit of error."

Hosea 5:15..."I will go and return to My place, till they acknowledge their offense, and seek My Face: in their affliction they will seek Me early."

Hosea 6:1-3, 6....Come, and let us return unto the Lord: for He hath torn, and He will heal us; He hast smitten, and He will bind us up. After two days will He revive us: in the third day He will raise us up, and we shall live in His sight. Then shall we know, if we follow on to know the Lord: His going forth is prepared as the morning; and He shall come unto us as the rain, as the latter and former rain unto the earth. For I desired mercy, and not sacrifice; and the knowledge of God more than burnt offerings."

Isaiah 59:1-4..."Behold, the Lord's hand is not shortened, that it cannot save; neither His ear heavy, that it cannot hear: BUT your iniquities have separated between you and your God, and your sins have hid His face from you, that He will not hear. For your hands are defiled with blood, and your fingers with iniquity; your lips have spoken lies, your tongue hath muttered perverseness. None calleth for justice, nor any pleadeth for truth: they trust in vanity, and speak lies; they conceive mischief, and bring forth iniquity."

2 Corinthians 7:1...Having therefore these promises, dearly beloved, let us cleanse ourselves from all filthiness of the flesh and spirit, perfecting holiness in the fear of God."

CHAPTER 17 Mystery of Iniquity Revealed the Cleansing of the Heart Idols

Many prophetic people believe we have entered into the "Days of Noah", beginning in 1997 when the comet Hale-Bopp, for the second time entered earth's viewing. The last time this comet was seen from our planet, was during the time of Noah, when he was building the ark.

What is iniquity? It is different than sin. Sin is the "fruit of iniquity". So iniquity has to do with the "roots of the sin".

Remember when Jesus talked about a tree? Matthew 7:15-20-27... "Beware of false prophets, which come to you in sheep's clothing, but inwardly they are ravening wolves. Ye shall know them by their fruits. Do men gather grapes of thorns, or figs of thistles? Even so every good tree brings forth good fruit; but a corrupt tree brings forth evil fruit. A good tree cannot bring forth evil fruit, neither can a corrupt tree bring forth good fruit. Every tree that brings not forth good fruit is hew down, and cast into the fire. Wherefore by their fruits ye shall know them. Not every one that saith unto me, Lord, Lord, shall enter into the kingdom of heaven; but he that does the will of My Father, which is in heaven. Many will say to Me in that day, Lord, Lord, have we not prophesied in Thy Name? and in Thy Name have cast out devils? and in Thy Name done many wonderful works? And then will I profess unto them, I never knew you: depart from Me, ye that work iniquity.

24...Therefore whosoever hears these sayings of mine, and does them, I will liken him unto a wise man, which built his house upon a rock: and the rains descended, and the floods came, and the winds blew, and beat upon that house; and it fell not: for it was founded upon a rock: 26.. And every one that hears these sayings of mine, and does NOT do them, shall be likened unto a foolish man, which built his house upon the sand: And the rains descended, and the floods came, and the winds blew, and beat upon that house; and it fell: and great was the fall of it."

James 1:21-22..."Wherefore lay apart all filthiness and superfluity of naughtiness, and receive with meekness the engrafted word, which is able to save your souls. BUT be ye doers of the word, and not hearers only, deceiving your own selves."

The first time iniquity is mentioned, it had to do with Lucifer - Satan in his fall. Ezekiel 28:15-18...

"Thou wast perfect in thy ways from the day that thou was created, till iniquity was found in thee.

By the multitude of thy merchandise they have filled the midst of thee with violence, and thou hast sinned: therefore I will cast thee as profane out of the mountain of God: and I will destroy thee, O

covering cherub, for the midst of the stones of fire. Thine heart was lifted up because of thy beauty, thou hast corrupted thy wisdom by reason of thy brightness: I will cast thee to the ground, I will lay thee before kings, that they may behold thee. Thou hast defiled thy sanctuaries by the multitude of thine iniquities, by the iniquity of thy traffic........

The Lord God spoke to Abram during the cutting of the covenant with him. Genesis 15:16..."But in the fourth generation they shall come hither again: for the iniquity of the Amorites is not yet full."

The Lord God also spoke to Moses regarding iniquity, when Moses desired to see the Glory of the Lord.

Exodus 34:6, 7...And the Lord passed by before him, and proclaimed, The Lord, The Lord God, merciful and gracious, long-suffering, and abundant in goodness and truth, Keeping mercy for thousands, forgiving iniquity and transgression and sin, and that will by no means clear the guilty; visiting the iniquity of the fathers upon the children, and upon the children's children, unto the third and to the fourth generation." Exodus 34:9..."And he said, If now I have found grace in thy sight, O Lord let my Lord, I pray thee, go among us; for it is a stiff-necked people; and pardon our iniquity and our sin, and take us for thine inheritance."

Our Lord bore the penalty of iniquity for us and became a curse for us: Isaiah 53:5, 6.... "But He was wounded for our transgressions, He was bruised for our iniquities: the chastisement of our peace was upon Him; and with His stripes we are healed. All we like sheep have gone astray; we have turned everyone to his own way; and the Lord hath laid on Him the iniquity of us all."

Proverbs 4:23, 24.... "Keep thy heart with all diligence; for out of it are the issues of life. Put away from thee a froward mouth and perverse lips put far from thee."

Mark 7: 13-23... "Making the Word of God of none effect through your tradition, which ye have delivered: and many such like things ye do. And when He had called all the people unto Him, He said unto them, Hearken unto me every one of you, and understand: There is nothing from without a man that entering into him can defile him: but the things which come out of him, those are they that defile the man. If any man have ears to hear, let him hear. And when he was entered into the house from the people, his disciples asked Him concerning the parable. And He saith unto them, Are ye so without understanding also? Do ye not perceive, that whatsoever thing from without enters into the man, it cannot defile him; because it enters not into his heart, but into the belly and goes out into the draught,

purging all meats? And He said, That which comes out of the man, that defiles the man. For from within, out of the heart of men, proceed evil thoughts, adulteries, fornications, murders, thefts, covetousness, wickedness, deceit, lasciviousness, an evil eye, blasphemy, pride, foolishness. Al these evil things come from within, and defile the man."

Peter's Denial an Example of Iniquity: Mark 8:29-33..."And He saith unto them, But whom say ye that I am? And Peter answers and saith unto Him, Thou art the Christ. And He charged them that they should tell no man of Him. And He began to teach them, that the Son of man must suffer many things, and be rejected of the elders, and of the chief priest, and scribes, and be killed, and after three days rise again. And He spake that saying openly, And Peter took Him, and began to rebuke Him.

But when He had turned about and looked on His disciples, He rebuked Peter, saying, Get thee behind me Satan: for thou savourest not the things that be of God, but the things that be of men."

Peter's denial is an example of iniquity working in one who follows the Lord Jesus. Peter, through the Spirit, was given the revelation of Jesus Christ, but then when Jesus began to share about what was soon to take place in His life, Peter pulls Him aside and rebukes Him. Then Jesus, speaking directly to Satan in Peter, rebukes that spirit of iniquity in Peter, named "Satan".

This is a perfect example of "dead flies in the ointment" - an evil mixture within the heart of His people. A double-minded man has two kingdoms battling within him. The Kingdom of Light, and the Kingdom of Darkness, i.e. lies from the father of lies, about the character of Jesus Christ and His Heavenly Father.

Remember what the Word says about being double-minded? James 1:8… "A double minded man is unstable in all his ways." James 4:8…"Draw nigh to God, and He will draw nigh to you. Cleanse

your hands, ye sinners; and purify your hearts, ye double-minded."

Proverbs 23:7….For as he thinks in his heart, so is he: Eat and drink, saith he to thee; but his heart is not with thee."

These scriptures deal with much deeper issues in the believer than have been traditionally taught. They are uncovering the condition of the human heart of unbelief. Hebrew 3:12…"Take heed, brethren, lest there be in any of you an evil heart of unbelief, in departing from the living God."

Psalm 50:16, 17, 19, 20,21, 22, 23…. "But unto the wicked God says, What hast thou to do to declare my statutes, or that thou should take my covenant in thy mouth? Seeing thou hates instruction, and casts My words behind thee. Thou gives thy mouth to evil, and thy tongue frames deceit. Thou sits and speaks against thy brother; thou slanders thine own mother's son. These things hast thou done, and I kept silence; thou thought that I was altogether such an one as thyself: but I will reprove thee, and set them in order before thine eyes. Now consider this, ye that forget God, lest I tear you in pieces, and there be none to deliver. Whoso offers praise glorifies Me: and to him that orders his conversation (his life) aright will I show the salvation of God."

Psalm 17:2, 4, 15... "Thou hast proved mine heart; thou hast visited me in the night; thou hast tried me, and shalt find nothing; I am purposed that my mouth shall not transgress. Concerning the works of men, by the Word of thy lips I have kept me from the paths of the destroyer...As for me, I will behold thy face in righteousness: I shall be satisfied, when I awake, to Thy likeness."

John 4:23-24... "But the hour comes, and now is, when the true worshippers shall worship the Father in spirit and in truth: for the Father seeks such to worship Him. God is a Spirit: and they that worship Him must worship Him in spirit and in truth."

John 3:17-21...For God sent NOT His Son into the world to condemn the world; but that the world through Him might be saved. He that believes on Him is not condemned: but he that believes not is condemned already, because he has not believed in the Name of the only begotten Son of God.

And this is the condemnation (judgment), that light is come into the world, and men loved darkness rather than light, because their deeds were evil. For every one that does evil hates the light, neither comes to the light, lest his deeds should be reproved. <u>BUT he that does truth comes to the light, that his deeds may be made manifest, that they are wrought in God.</u>"

John 8:29.... "<u>And He that sent Me is with Me: the Father hath not left Me alone; for I do always those things that please Him. " This is the KEY scripture!!!!!!! Jesus always did what Pleased The Heavenly Father. And this is what we are to focus on....pleasing the Father in spirit, soul (mind, will and emotions) and our bodies. His pleasure, not ours!.</u>

John 8:30-32..._ "As He spake these words, many believed on Him. Then said Jesus to those Jews which believed on Him, IF ye continue in My Words, then are ye my disciples indeed: And ye shall know the truth, and the truth shall make you free."

John 15:14... "Ye are my friends, IF ye do whatsoever I command you."

Remember in the Word where Jesus said: "Satan came to Me, But found nothing in Me." Jesus was speaking of iniquity. There was no iniquity in Jesus. He knew the Father completely, and all His heart was filled with truth and love of and for the Heavenly Father. Jesus' heart had no unbelief, no hidden lies He was believing of the Father. Thus, Jesus worshipped the Father in completeness and wholeness in His spirit. He only did what The Father showed Him to do. He only spoke what He heard The Father speak. John 5:30..."I can of mine own self do nothing; as I hear, I judge: and My judgment is just; because I seek not mine own will, but the will of the Father which hath sent me."

This is where the Body of Christ is heading! We are going to become His Body, as He walked on this earth; seeking ONLY the Father's pleasure and heart; and DOING only what the Father shows and says.

BUT this is going to take a cleansing fire that His Body, at this point, isn't embracing or even believing.

I have heard "countless" believers calling on the "FIRE OF GOD", and they do not know what they are asking. They are calling on a "false fire", not one of cleansing.

Malachi 3:1-3...Behold, I will send my messenger, and he shall prepare the way before Me; and the Lord, whom ye seek, shall suddenly come to His Temple (His Body of Believers), even the messenger of the covenant, whom ye delight in: behold he shall come, saith the Lord of Host. BUT who may abide the day of His coming? and who shall stand when He appears? for He is like a refiner's fire, and fullers' soap: And He shall sit as a refiner and purifier of silver: and He shall purify the sons of Levi, and purge them as gold and silver, that they may offer unto the Lord an offering in righteousness."

(Laodicea Church - "cleansing by fire" - brings forth "true faith tried by fire.")

Ephesians 6:26-27..... "even as Christ also loved the church, and gave Himself for it; That He might sanctify and cleanse it with the washing of water by the word, That He might present it to Himself a glorious church, not having spot, or wrinkle, or any such thing; but that it should be holy and without blemish."

Jesus has declared that He is coming back for a glorious church. One in which each stone (living stones) has a pure heart for Him, just like

He had a pure heart for the Father, while He walked this earth to the cross. Matthew 5:8..."Blessed are the pure in heart; for they shall see God."

1 John 3:2, 3... "Beloved, now are we the sons of God, and it doth not yet appear what we shall be: but we know that, when He shall appear, we shall be like Him; for we shall see Him as He is. AND every man that hath this hope in him purifies himself, even as He is pure."

2 Thessalonians 1:10... "When He shall come to be glorified IN His saints, and to be admired in all them that believe (because our testimony among you was believed) in that day.

Ezekiel 14:3...Son of man, these men have set up their idols in their heart, and put the stumbling block of their iniquity before their face...Ezekiel 14:6..."Thus saith the Lord God; Repent, and turn yourselves from your idols; and turn your faces from all your abominations."

Now, to all those that are saying: "These are Old Testament scriptures." - The Word states:

Hebrews 2:1-3... "Therefore we ought to give the more earnest heed to the things which we have heard, lest at any time we should let them slip. For if the word spoken by angels was stedfast, and every transgression and disobedience received a just recompense of reward; How shall we escape, if we neglect so great salvation; which at first began to be spoken by the Lord, and was confirmed unto us by them that heard Him;"

What I am going to share is not a popular teaching among the Body of Christ, yet it is time to be shared. And hopefully, those of you that truly want to be completely free, completely whole, and only be subject to the Holy Spirit - filled with the fullness of God, will have ears to hear what the Spirit is saying.

We are in the time of the Laodicea church spoken of in Revelation 3:14-22. We know that this is a type of the end time church and we are familiar with what is written. "I know thy works, that thou art neither cold nor hot: I would thou wert cold or hot. So then because thou art lukewarm, and neither cold nor hot, I will spue thee out of my mouth. Because you say, I am rich, and increased with goods, and have need of nothing; and know not that thou art wretched, and miserable, and poor, and blind, and naked: I counsel thee to buy of me gold tried in the fire, that thou may be rich; and white raiment, that tho may be clothed, and that the shame of thy nakedness do not appear; and anoint thine eyes with eyesalve, that thou may see. As many as I love, I rebuke and chasten: be zealous therefore, and repent.

Behold, I stand at the door, and knock: if any man hear my voice, and open the door, I will come in to him, and will sup with him, and he with me. To him that overcomes will I grant to sit with me in my throne, even as I also overcame, and am set down with my Father in his throne. He that hath an ear let him hear what the Spirit says unto the churches."

Matthew 25 speaks of the five wise virgins and five foolish virgins. We are in that time now.

The scripture of Jesus knocking on the door has been used as an invitation to be saved, which is fine, but that is not the context of what is spoken here. He is standing "outside" of the believer's heart, the place where He has not had access, where hidden idols are lodged. He is desperately wanting to enter in so that the Strong Man of the house can be bound and his goods spoiled.

We have been taught that the Holy Spirit cannot dwell in the same place as evil- in the same heart. But throughout scripture, the only way evil can be expelled is when the Stronger One - The Spirit of the Lord, i.e. Holy Spirit comes in and by His Peace, binds the strong man and casts him out.

Romans 16:20... "And the God of peace shall bruise Satan under your feet shortly......"

Isaiah 10:27... "And it shall come to pass in that day, that his burden shall be taken away from off thy shoulder, and his yoke from off thy neck, and the yoke shall be destroyed because of the anointing."

How do heart idols come about? When and how does a person set up an idol in the inner chambers of his being? And what effect does having an idol do to the person, to his relationship with the Lord Jesus Christ, and to those closest to him, his family? Before I answer these important questions, I would like to share a vision the Lord gave me back in 1990, in Boulder, Colorado, while I was attending a full gospel worship service.

THE VISION I HAD IN BOULDER, COLORADO 1990

As I was worshipping the Lord, He unveiled something in the spirit realm that had a life changing impact on me - thus this book being birthed!

The actual church service was filled to capacity. I had my eyes closed while we were all singing, and then the "vision" took place. This is what He showed me in the spirit realm regarding everyone in that church service. EVERY SINGLE PERSON THERE WAS HOLDING IN THEIR HANDS, RESTING IN THEIR LAPS, A WHITE STATUE, AN IDOL.

I knew I had one too, but had NO idea what it was I was holding in my hands. That vision stayed with me and I asked the Holy Spirit to teach me what this meant, for me and for the Body of Christ.

He is faithful to teach and to bring us into all truth. The Lord has since shown me the truth about heart idols in everyone, believers and non-believers, alike.

The idols - belief systems - passed down through generations that are riddled with unbelief and lies about the true character of the Living God, which started in the Garden with our first father and mother, Adam and Eve. These belief systems then manifest into rebellion and disobedience, which causes the "curse of the law" to transpire in an individual, in families, in nations, and even church fellowships. And they continue to be passed down, UNTIL the Truth is embraced, and then there can be true freedom and deliverance!

CHAPTER 18 Heart Idols Set Up In Childhood

Idols are set up in childhood. Children do not have the coping skills in the Spirit, and are very vulnerable to the lies of Satan, especially during a traumatic time; a time of loss, a time of deep disappointment, violence whether physical or verbal. One thing about a child, they DO KNOW, in their spirit, who or what their parents worship, even in the womb. Jeremiah 17: 1,2..."The sin of Judah is written with a pen of iron, and with the point of a diamond: it is graven upon the table of their heart, and upon the horns of your alters; While their children remember their altars and their groves by the green trees upon the hills."

Jeremiah 17:9, 10..."The heart is deceitful above all things and desperately wicked: who can know it? I the Lord search the heart, I try the reins, even to every man according to his ways, and according to the fruit of his doings."

Idols ALWAYS are rooted in OFFENSE TOWARDS THE LORD, through the lies that have been believed, and they are wrapped in the demonic, to give the idol power.

The child's heart becomes offended at God. It all goes back to Satan lying about the character of the True and Living God. When a child believes the inner lie about God, that He is not a Good God, nor can He be trusted, or that God was the One who hurt him; the child will not trust God. He will turn to something he "thinks" he can trust, and thus idolatry is setup. Then Satan is given legal right to introduce to the child evil spirits, and a strong hold is set in place. Children do look to their earthly fathers as a picture of the Heavenly Father. The Lord set it up that way, and we know that, particularly in this generation, that truth speaks volumes.

I have had countless people tell me about their parents, or them, actually listening and even "playing" with demons when they were young. This occurs more than anyone knows, or wants to admit, especially in the Body of Christ.

Therefore, this takes place deep within a child. Then, when the person accepts Jesus Christ as Savior, the process of sanctification begins. Now this is where the "rubber meets the road".

A believer continues along and loves the Lord, obeys His commands, UNTIL a situation occurs that touches that "childhood pain", which houses the heart idol. Then as we have seen more often than not, even in my own life, the believer falls, gets back up, falls again, and so forth.

Eventually, the Holy Spirit confronts the believer, or tries to, if the believer truly wants to be made whole and deal with the pain and PAY THE PRICE of getting free; he will get free. It's the believer's choice.

This is where I have seen so many people in the body of Christ, back up, and say: "No thank you Lord. I want to stay in my comfort zone, and not die to the flesh, face the terrible pain and go on with You; being changed from Glory to Glory." Many in the body of Christ want to continue in the works of the flesh because there is a deep reward and satisfaction in doing so. The Lord told me: "This is called, Unholy justification." Deep in the person's heart, they do not want to forgive, they want revenge, they want to stay the victim, and they want "other people's oil." They like their sin! They do not choose to suffer affection with the people of God; rather they choose to "enjoy the pleasures of sin for a season."

At the point in a person's heart where he is the most deeply offended at the Lord, a choice is made in the person's spirit. When the Holy Spirit confronts that person regarding the deep things of God, the believer makes the choice. The decision to continue to believe the lie about the character of God OR to go on and Trust the Lord at His Word, by hearing and obeying. If the person does not want to take God at His Word, he will turn and continue walking in the flesh (which dwells no good thing -

Romans 7:18..."For I know that in me (that is, in my flesh) dwells no good thing....." And then "RELIGION" is then set up in that person. Having a form of godliness, but denying the power thereof, from such turn away.

I might add, that truly the Lord is The God of mercy and is long suffering towards us. Psalm 16:6..."By mercy and truth iniquity is purged: and by the fear of the Lord men depart from evil."

Adam and Eve listened to Satan and sewed "religious coverings", fig leaves to cover their iniquity, instead of repenting to the Lord and confessing their bitterness towards Him. They were deceived, and then they blamed God and became bitter. Job 31:33..."If I covered my transgressions as Adam, by hiding my iniquity in my bosom...(heart).."

By having an idol, the "spirit of whoredoms" is given place which causes error.

Then that spirit ushers in the "spirit of anti-christ" which sets up religion in a person, a family, a church, a nation.

That's why the Word of God declares in 2 Timothy 2:19-22... "Nevertheless the foundation of God stands sure, having this seal, The Lord knows them that are his.

And, Let everyone that names the name of Christ depart from iniquity. But in a great house there are not only vessels of gold and silver, but also wood and of earth: and some to honor, and some to dishonor. If a man therefore purge himself from these, he shall be a vessel unto honor, sanctified, and meet for the master's use, and prepared unto every good work. Flee also youthful lusts: but follow righteousness, faith, charity, peace, with them that call on the Lord out of a pure heart."

2 Timothy 2:24-26..."And the servant of the Lord must not strive; but be gentle unto all men, apt to teach, patient, In meekness instructing those that oppose themselves; if God peradventure will give them repentance to the acknowledging of the truth; And that they may recover themselves out of the snare of the devil, who are taken captive by him at his will."

Jeremiah 18:2-6... "Arise, and go down to the potter's house, and there I will cause thee to hear My words. Then I went down to the potter's house, and, behold he wrought a work on the wheels. And the vessel that he made of clay was marred in the hand of the potter: so he made it again another vessel, as seemed good to the potter to make it."

A story I heard some time ago about a potter's work...I was in Colorado, listening to a Christian station out of Golden, when I heard this testimony of a man who was a missionary in the Orient. Here was his story.

He said: "The Lord woke him up one day and gave him the scripture in Jeremiah about the potter's house. Then the Lord spoke to the missionary to go to a potter in the local village.

Therefore, the missionary got up, and went to the Village Potter.

The missionary followed the potter around and watched what he did. The potter first went to a shed at the back of his property and scooped out the blackest, stench of goop he had ever seen. He took that "black junk" and threw it on his potter wheel and began turning it on the wheel, along with a continual flow of water. The potter was shaping that stuff with his gentle hands. Every now and then, the potter would stop the wheel and pull out debris - rocks, sticks, hay, etc., things that were lodged in the goop of clay. His hands would feel the roughness as he turned the wheel with the water. Then he would continue to shape, what became a beautiful object.

As the missionary wandered around the potter's shop, he noticed all types of vessels. Some were the most beautiful goblets he had seen.

Some were pretty bowls, and yet some vessels looked like just ordinary, plain old pots, something a person might use as an ash tray, or even a spittoon. The missionary asked the potter why he made the vessels so diverse. The potter answered: "The ordinary, plain vessels gave me too much resistance!"

What more can be added to this very strong, visual Word of the Lord? He is faithful and merciful, BUT there is a line that can be crossed with the Spirit of the Lord at some point in each of our lives.

To me, that is the most FRIGHTENING thing that could happen.

The Lord has spoken to me, and I know He has spoken and shown others this Word too, and that is:

"The time of Ananias and Sapphire will come back in the Church before it's over."

He needs to get us BACK to where the first Church was, and then He will take us farther than we can even imagine. And His Body will, as stated in John 14:12... "Verily, verily I say unto you, He that believes on Me, the works that I do shall he do also; and greater works than these shall he do; because I go unto my Father."

CHAPTER 19 The Jonah Principle

The Lord has brought the story Jonah, and the sign of Jonah, to me, many times in these past 27 years. It is a multifaceted prophecy AND sign, to us, now. AND a WORD OF WARNING, to each of us. - The "spirit of Jonah" = disobedience and the absence of the Love of God!

Matthew 16:4... "A wicked and adulterous generation seeks after a sign; and there shall be no sign be given unto it, but the sign of the prophet Jonah. And He left them and departed."

Jonah 1:6-10... "So the shipmaster came to him (Jonah), and said unto him, What meanest thou, O sleeper? arise, call upon thy God, if so be that God will think upon us, that we perish not.

And they said everyone to his fellow, Come, and let us cast lots, that we may know for whose cause this evil is upon us. So they cast lots, and the lot fell upon Jonah.

Then said they unto him, Tell us, we pray thee, for whose cause this is upon us; What is thine occupation? and whence comest thou?

109

what is thy country? and of what people are thou?

And he said unto them, I am an Hebrew; and I fear the LORD, the God of heaven, which hath made the sea and the dry land. Then were the men exceedingly afraid, and said unto him; Why hast thou done this? For the men knew that he fled from the presence of the Lord, because he had told them......

(We know the story of Jonah and the fish........)

Jonah 4:8-11..."And it came to pass, when the sun did arise, that God prepared a vehement east wind; and the sun beat upon the head of Jonah, that he fainted, and wished in himself to die, and said: It is better for me to die than live. And God said to Jonah, Doest thou well to be angry for the gourd? And he said, I do well to be angry, even unto death. Then said the LORD, Thou hast had pity on the gourd, for the which thou hast not labored, neither made it grow; which came up in a night, and perished in a night: And should not I spare Nineveh, that great city, wherein are more than six-score thousand persons that cannot discern between their right hand and their left hand (120,000 very little children); and also much cattle?

Ezekiel 33:11... "Say unto them, As I live, saith the Lord God, I have no pleasure in the death of the wicked; but that the wicked turn from his way and live: turn ye, turn ye from your evil ways; for why will ye die, O house of Israel?"

I believe, we as the Church, are in this time now, when the Spirit of the Lord is calling each of us "out" of the whoredoms.

We, each individually must be brought to the place of Perfect LOVE, by His Spirit- broken, humble, sacrificial, unconditional Love, before the Lord of Glory, can trust us with His Power!!!!!!!!!!!!!!

I Corinthians 13:1-3... "Though I speak with the tongues of men and of angels, and have not charity, I am become as sounding brass, or a tinkling cymbal. And though I have the gift of prophecy, and understand all mysteries, and all knowledge; and though I have faith, so that I could remove mountains, and have not charity, I am nothing. And though I bestow all my goods to feed the poor, and though I give my body to be burned, and have not charity, it profiiteth me nothing...."

Jonah "ran" from the Presence of the Lord God, because he didn't have "Love" for his enemies. AND, it actually caused the storm that was going to destroy, not only him, but also the heathen, the unbelievers who didn't "know" the Lord, King of the Universe.

Today, in America, the Church is pointing fingers at "the heathen, those trapped in darkness", including "our leaders". Hate filled speech, bashing, is the norm; "thinking" that it's (the people in darkness) their fault that is bringing judgment to this nation. Look at ancient Covenant Israel for the pattern of judgment and why.

That is total and complete ERROR! What does the Word declare: 2 Chronicles 7:13-14...IF I shut up heaven that there be no rain, or if I command the locusts to devour the land, or if I send pestilence among my people;

IF MY PEOPLE, WHICH ARE CALLED BY MY NAME, SHALL HUMBLE THEMSELVES, AND PRAY, AND SEEK MY FACE, AND TURN FROM THEIR WICKED WAYS; then will I hear from heaven, and will forgive their sin, and will heal their land."

We hear this verse quoted SO OFTEN in our fellowships and on T.V. BUT they STOP at

"PRAY"........This verse is calling His People to Repent from THEIR WICKED WAYS.

It is OUR FAULT, (just like it was Jonah's fault - his running in disobedience from a direct command from Heaven), that the judgments are falling on this land of the United States!!!!!!!!!!!!!!!!!!!!!!!!!!!!!!

The Lord Jesus Christ gave His Church the responsibility of being "light and salt", not the heathen. And He gave a very solemn warning to His People: 1 Peter 4:17..."For the time is come that judgment must begin at the house of God: and if it first begin in us, what shall the end be of them that obey not the gospel of God?"

HEAVEN IS PLEADING with His People, especially the Leaders, to turn completely to Him, and allow Him to be LORD - KING COMPLETELY. The world is dying and going to hell.! And great sorrow is on the horizon of this nation and world. We need to get ready by rending our hearts, and not our garments. The Prophecy of Joel is getting ready to take place.

This is what I have "seen and experienced" in His Body, and what He is calling us, individually, out from:

Revelation 18:4..."And I heard another voice from heaven saying, Come out of her, MY PEOPLE, that ye be not partakers of her sins, and that ye receive not of her plagues".——the Great Harlot, Mystery Babylon - the whoredoms of the heart, and of nations, run by human hearts!

Witchcrafts in the Body of Christ:

This is what the Lord shared regarding the witchcrafts in the Body of Christ. The witchcraft spirit operates like this: a person who, in one way or another has been a victim of some sorts, (and we all have at some level) and has become offended in their heart with God, so they won't trust Him on some level of their being - a very, very deep wound and offense, not in their conscience, but in their sub conscience.

The "believer" wants, needs, and even lusts after personal power. And so instead of turning to Jesus Christ and willingly trust Him and His Power via His Word to fix it, they are deceived by a spirit of whoredoms, set up in childhood. That "spirit", which is actually an anti-christ spirit tries to destroy through pollution (a mixture of truth and error) (dead flies in the ointment) the anointing in that person's life and in others. The believer actually draws power from that spirit, unknowingly.

The Satanist's use and call on spirits of witchcraft, openly, face to face, knowingly. But in the Church, that spirit is "masked" looking pure and holy, false light appearing to be real.

Jesus says in Matthew 6:21-23... "For where your treasure is, there will your heart be also. The light of the body is the eye: if therefore thine eye be single, thy whole body shall be full of light.

But if thine eye be evil (foggy - how you perceive in your heart), thy whole body shall be full of darkness, how great is that darkness!" It is great darkness because the "light" that we "think" we see, is actually, perverted truth, which becomes gross deception....You cannot serve God and Money!. Who do you trust? Where is your heart on this matter?

========================
=========================
=========================
==

The "GREATEST THING" that I have been "judged" by in these last 27 years, following the Lord of Hosts where ever AND HOW EVER, He leads...is the money issue, or lack thereof.

People in the Body have treated and thought of me less because of the "issue of money"....even by those who knew that I was called out "on the Water" taking Him at His Word only, that HE WILL SUPPLY MY EVERY NEED. (Truly the Lord has uncovered "many" money changers in His Body, by having me walk such an "upside down walk" being a spectacle to the world, and to angels, and to men. And let me go on record.....He HAS supplied every need, not on my time, BUT HIS: and truly He is the Faithful and True One coming in the Clouds of Glory. Will He find "Faith on the Earth" Laodicea Church?

=======================
=======================
=======================
====

And how "self-righteous" we are because we believe we are walking in the light, when we are actually in gross darkness. That is why religious people are the HARDEST to deal with because they think they are pure.

Proverbs 30:12..."There is a generation that are pure in their own eyes, and yet is not washed from their filthiness."

Satan is called the "angel of light". He deceives by perverting the light of truth. Isn't it interesting that Jezebel's name means: "unmarried, chaste". And chaste in the dictionary means: "Morally pure in thought or conduct; decent and modest".

Witchcraft is a work of the flesh. If a person has not dealt with dying to "self" power (soul power), that person can become a sounding brass, or a tinkling cymbal; speaking truth, but not out of love by the Holy Spirit's unction. (The letter of the law, which kills.)

That is why the "spirit of religion", false ministry spirits, (Babylon), have so wounded the Lord's Body. Deceiving through the traditions of men, passed down through twisting the Living Word, causing sorrow to His people, and actually, in some very tragic cases, bringing about "spiritual abortions".

Ezekiel 14:5... "That I may take Israel in their own heart, because they are all estranged from Me through their idols." Ezekiel 6:9, 10..."And they that escape of you shall remember Me among the nations whither they shall be carried captives, because "I am broken with their whorish heart, which hath departed from Me, and with their eyes, which go a whoring after their idols; and they shall loathe themselves for the evils which they have committed in all their abominations. And they shall know that I AM the Lord, and that I have not said in vain that I would do this evil unto them."

Jeremiah 4:18.... "Break up your fallow ground, and sow not among thorns."

Jeremiah 4 14... "Wash thine heart from wickedness, that thou mayest be saved. How long shall thy vain thoughts lodge within thee?"

James 4:8... "Draw nigh to God, and He will draw night to you. Cleanse your hands, ye sinners; and purify hour hearts, ye double minded."

Babylon is described in Habakkuk 1:6..."For, lo, I raise up the Chaldeans, that bitter and hasty nation, which shall march through the breadth of the land, to possess the dwelling places that are not their's."

Remember, throughout scripture, The Lord has always used a heathen nation for judgment on His People. His Word remains unchanged......and the "terrorists are from that region.

He IS LOVE, and our whorish hearts, bring destruction into our lives and families, and it breaks His Heart. He longs to bring His Life and His Love to people. He took it all for us, and yet we bind Him and His loving arms through an evil heart of unbelief. And we continually reject His desperate wooing of us to willingly obey His instructions.

Psalm 139:23-24… "Search me, O God, and know my heart: try me, and know my thoughts: And see if there be any wicked way in me, and lead me in the way everlasting."

2 Corinthians 6:1… "Having therefore these promises, dearly beloved, let us cleanse ourselves from all filthiness of the flesh and spirit, perfecting holiness in the fear of God."

Here is the million-dollar question, and answer for His Children! Why don't the children of the Most High God walk completely in the Spirit, being led of Him every step of the way?

Because in order to be "led", we first must trust who is leading. And this is where the whoredoms of the heart which has set up the idols, manifests -disobedience!

Remember, it is the "little foxes that eat the vines". There is a law in the Spirit realm, that whosoever is faithful in the least, will be faithful in the greater". If the person, continually neglects the "smallest unction's of the Holy

Spirit, either by the written Word or the Still Small Voice, he will not obey when the Lord is directing him from REAL DANGER.

CHAPTER 20 True Story of Not Obeying a Simple Instruction from the Lord

A pastor and his family were traveling. They had stopped overnight in a motel room. In the morning, the Lord instructed the pastor to "wait 30 minutes before leaving". The pastor disregarded the instruction of the Holy Spirit, by an obvious decision, he left, and didn't wait the 30 minutes.

Proverbs 1:25... "But ye have set at nought all my counsel, and would none of my reproof:"

Proverbs 29:25... "The fear of man brings a snare: but whoso putts his trust in the Lord shall be safe."

Proverbs 1:33... "But whoso hearkens unto Me shall dwell safely, and shall be quiet from fear of evil."

SO THE PASTOR and his wife and his children left. They hadn't been on the highway for very long, when they were HIT HEAD ON by a drunk driver!. The pastor was the only person that survived the crash.

He lost his entire family because of disobeying a simple command!

I weep again, even now, when I write this story. The Father weeps too, because this is NOT what He planned for this family. But because His instruction was cast behind the back, tragedy struck.

AND then Satan uses this tragedy, which struck a believer, to lie about the Father's character, again, and His love for us; AND even whether or not, the Lord of Hosts is even capable of protecting His children. And our Heavenly Father gets blamed again, even if it is not spoken, about whether He is truly the loving Father.

My brothers and sisters, this ought not to be so.

CHAPTER 21 A Lesson and a Warning

Corrie Ten Boom's View on the Rapture Teaching

Ezekiel 33:1 - 7.... "Again, the Word of the Lord came unto me, saying,

Son of Man, speak to the children of thy people, and say unto them, When I bring the sword upon a land, if the people of the land take a man of their coasts, and set him for their watchman: If when he sees the sword come upon the land, he blow the trumpet, and warn the people; Then whosoever hears the sound of the trumpet, and takes not warning; if the sword come, and take him away, his blood shall be upon him. But he that takes warning shall deliver his soul.

But if the watchman see the sword come, and blow not the trumpet, and people be not warned; if the sword come, and take away any person, from among them, he is taken away in his iniquity; but his blood will I require at the watchman's hand. So thou, O son of man, I have set thee a watchman unto the house of Israel; therefore thou shalt hear the word at My mouth, and warn them from Me."

==========================
===========================
===========================
======

What happened in the church in Europe during World War II, is a parallel story behind the undeniable horror of the Holocaust. While there were countless heroes who risked everything; it is clear that the majority of the church in Europe, was totally unprepared for the horrors of Nazi Germany; many believers even "falling away" as a result of the proliferation of a "pre-tribulation rapture" doctrine.

Corrie Ten Boom spoke openly of multitudes who turned from the faith during the Nazi's Holocaust of World War II. She related how preachers were besieged with parishioners questioning them as to why they had falsely taught them that there would be a "pre-tribulation rapture", and why they didn't, instead, warn them to become spiritually prepared for tribulation. Corrie testified of how she personally witnessed persecuted Christians turn from the faith because they had expected to escape by a "secret rapture". They were caught unaware and unprepared for suffering and martyrdom. Corrie Ten Boom, a precious saint - now present with the Lord -

personally suffered for Jesus. She strongly warned Christians to get their eyes off of any rapture before the Tribulation.

The following letter was written by Ms. Corrie Ten Boom, a Nazi Concentration Camp survivor, and lifelong missionary, to many countries, in 1974. Here are excerpts from her letter of 1974:

"My sister, Betsy, and I were in the Nazi concentration camp at Ravensbruck because we committed the crime of loving Jews. Seven hundred of us from Holland, France, Russia, Poland and Belgium were herded into a room built for two hundred. As far as I knew, Betsy and I were the only two representatives of Heaven in that room. We may have been the Lord's only representatives in that place of hatred, yet because of our presence there, things changed. Jesus said, "In the world you shall have tribulation; but be of good cheer, I have overcome the world." We too, are to be overcomers - bringing the light of Jesus into a world filled with darkness and hate."

"Sometimes I get frightened as I read the Bible, and as I look in this world and see all of the tribulation and persecution promised by the Bible coming true."

"Betsy and I, in the concentration camp, prayed that God would heal Betsy who was so weak and sick. "Yes, the Lord will heal me," Betsy said with confidence. She died the next day and I could not understand it. They laid her thin body on the concrete floor along with all the other corpses of the women who died that day."

"It was hard for me to understand, to believe that God had a purpose for all that. Yet because of Betsy's death, today I am traveling all over the world telling people about Jesus."

"There are some among us teaching there will be no tribulation, that the Christians will be able to escape all this.

These are the false teachers that Jesus was warning us to expect in the latter days. Most of them have little knowledge of what is already going on across the world. I have been in countries where the saints are already suffering terrible persecution. In China, the Christians were told, "Don't worry, before the tribulation comes you will be translated - raptured."

Then came a terrible persecution; millions of Christians (20 million estimated martyrs) were tortured to death. Later I heard a Bishop from China say, sadly, "We have failed. We should have made the people strong for persecution rather than telling them Jesus would come first. Tell the people how to be strong in times of persecution, how to stand when the tribulation comes - to stand and not faint."

"I feel I have a divine mandate to go and tell the people of this world that it is possible to be strong in the Lord Jesus Christ. We are in training for the tribulation, but more than sixty percent of the Body of Christ across the world has already entered into the tribulation. There is no way to escape it. We are next."

"Since I have already gone through prison for Jesus' sake, and since I met the Bishop in China, now every time I read a good Bible text I think, "Hey, I can use that in the time of tribulation." Then I write it down and learn it by heart."

"When I was in the concentration camp, a camp where only twenty percent of the women came out alive, we tried to cheer each other up by saying, "Nothing could be any worse than today." But we would find the next day was even worse. During this time a Bible verse that I had committed to memory gave me great hope and joy. "If ye be reproached for the name of Christ, happy are ye; for the spirit of glory and of God resteth upon you; on their part evil is spoken of, but on your part He is glorified." (I Peter 3:14) I found myself saying, "Hallelujah! Because I am suffering, Jesus is glorified!"

"In America, the churches sing, "Let the congregation escape tribulation", but in China and Africa the tribulation has already arrived. This last year alone; more than two hundred thousand Christians were martyred in Africa. (1974)

Now things like that never get into the newspapers because they cause bad political relations. But I know. I have been there. We need to think about that when we sit down in our nice houses with our nice clothes to eat our steak dinners. Many, many members of the Body of Christ are being tortured to death at this very moment, yet we continue right on as though we are all going to escape the tribulation."

"Several years ago I was in Africa in a nation where a new government had come into power. The first night I was there some of the Christians were commanded to come to the police station to register. When they arrived they were arrested and that same night they were executed. The next day the same thing happened with other Christians. The third day it was the same. All the Christians in the district were being systematically murdered."

"The fourth day I was to speak in a little church. The people came, but they were filled with fear and tension. All during the service they were looking at each other, their eyes asking, "Will this one I am sitting beside be the next one killed? Will I be the next one?"

"When I was a little girl, "I said, "I went to my father and said, "Daddy, I am afraid that I will never be strong enough to be a martyr for Jesus Christ." "Tell me," said Father, "When you take a train trip to Amsterdam, when do I give you the money for the ticket? Three weeks before?" "No, Daddy, you give me the money for the ticket just before we get on the train." "That is right," my father said, "and so it is with God's strength. Our Father in Heaven knows when you will need the strength to be a martyr for Jesus Christ. He will supply all you need - just in time."

My African friends were nodding and smiling. Suddenly a spirit of joy descended upon that church and the people began singing, "In the sweet, by and by, we shall meet on that beautiful shore." Later that week, half the congregation of that church was executed. I heard later that the other half was killed some months ago."

"But I must tell you something. I was so happy that the Lord used me to encourage these people, for unlike many of their leaders, I had the word of God. I had been to the Bible and discovered that Jesus said He had not only overcome the world, but to all those who remained faithful to the end, He would give a crown of life."

"How can we get ready for the persecution? First, we need to feed on the word of God, digest it, and make it a part of our being. This will mean disciplined Bible study each day as we not only memorize long passages of scripture, but put the principles to work in our lives."

"Next we need to develop a personal relationship with Jesus Christ. Not just the Jesus of yesterday, the Jesus of History, but the life-changing Jesus of today who is still alive and sitting at the right hand of God."

"We must be filled with the Holy Spirit. This is no optional command of the Bible, it is absolutely necessary. Those earthly disciples could never have stood up under the persecution of the Jews and Romans had they not waited for Pentecost. Each of us needs our own personal Pentecost, the baptism of the Holy Spirit. We will never be able to stand in the tribulation without it."

"In the coming persecution we must be ready to help each other and encourage each other. However, we must not wait until the tribulation comes before starting. The fruit of the Spirit should be the dominant force of every Christian's life."

"Many are fearful of the coming tribulation, they want to run. I, too, am a little bit afraid when I think that after all my eighty years, including the horrible Nazi concentration camp; that I might have to go through the tribulation also. But then I read the Bible and I am glad."

"When I am weak, then I shall be strong, the Bible says. Betsy and I were prisoners for the Lord, we were so weak, but we got power because the Holy Spirit was on us. That mighty inner strengthening of the Holy Spirit helped us through. No, you will not be strong in yourself when the tribulation comes. Rather, you will be strong in the power of Him who will not forsake you. For seventy-six years I have known the Lord Jesus and not once has He ever left me, or let me down. Though He slay me, yet will I trust Him, for I know that to all who

overcome, He shall give the crown of life.
Hallelujah!

-Corrie Ten Boom-1974

www.ingramcontent.com/pod-product-compliance
Lightning Source LLC
Chambersburg PA
CBHW031321040426
42443CB00005B/166